The Pre-Reformation Church in England 1400–1530

REVISED EDITION

CHRISTOPHER HARPER-BILL

LONGMAN
LONDON AN

DR   C/R   X
/97   SHL
942·04
HAR

Addison Wesley Longman Limited
Edinburgh Gate
Harlow, Essex CM20 2JE, England
and associated Companies throughout the world.

Published in the United States of America
by Addison Wesley Longman Inc., New York.

First published 1989
Revised Edition 1996

ISBN 0 582 289890 PPR

British Library Cataloguing in Publication Data
A catalogue record of this book is
available from the British Library

Library of Congress Cataloging-in-Publication Data
Harper-Bill, Christopher.
  The pre-Reformation church in England, 1400–1530 / Christopher
Harper-Bill. – Rev. ed.
    p. cm. – (Seminar studies in history)
  Includes bibliographical references (p.) and index.
  ISBN 0-582-28989-0
  1. Catholic Church–England–History. 2. Catholic Church-
-England–History–16th century. 3. England–Church
history–1066–1485. 4. England–Church history–1485– 5. England-
-Church history–16th century. I. Title. II. Series.
BR750.H37 1996
282'.42'09024–dc20   96–4175
                                                                CIP

Set by 7 in 10/12 New Baskerville

Printed and bound in Great Britain by
Short Run Press Ltd, Exeter

Contents

Contents

EDITORIAL FOREWORD

Such is the pace of historical enquiry in the modern world that there is an ever-widening gap between the specialist article of monograph, incorporating the results of current research, and general surveys, which inevitably become out of date. *Seminar Studies in History* are designed to bridge this gap. The books are written by experts in their field who are not only familiar with the latest research but have often contributed to it. They are frequently revised, in order to take account of new information and interpretations. They provide a selection of documents to illustrate major themes and provoke discussion, and also a guide to further reading. Their aim is to clarify complex issues without over-simplifying them, and to stimulate readers into deepening their knowledge and understanding of major themes and topics.

ROGER LOCKYER

NOTE ON REFERENCING SYSTEM

Readers should note that numbers in square brackets [5] refer them to the corresponding entry in the Bibliography at the end of the book (specific page references are given in italics). A number in square brackets, preceded by *Doc* . [*Doc.* 5] refers readers to the corresponding item in the Documents section which follows the main text. Words which are defined in the Glossary are asterisked on their first occurrence in the book.

ACKNOWLEDGEMENTS

The Publishers would like to thank the following for permissions to reproduce copyright material:

The Bedfordshire Historical Record Society for an extract from *Bedfordshire Wills proved in the Prerogative Court of Canterbury 1383–1548*; The Royal Historical Society for an extract from *Camden, Third Series*, Vols XLV, XLVII and LIV; Her Majesty's Stationery Office for extracts from *The Papal Letters 1471–1484*; The Buckinghamshire Record Society for an extract from *The Courts of the Archdeaconry of Buckingham 1483–1523* by E.M. Elvey; The Canterbury and York Society for an extract from *Register of Richard Mayew, Bishop of Hereford* by A.T. Bannister (1921) and an extract from *Register of Charles Booth, Bishop of Hereford* by A.T. Bannister (1921); Penguin Books Ltd., Harmondsworth for an extract from *The Ladder of Perfection*, pp. 70–1 by Walter Hilton, translated by Leo Sherley-Price, published 1957, reproduced by permission of Penguin Books Ltd., Yale University Press for an extract from *Two Early Tudor Lives*, edited by R.S. Sylvester and D.P. Harding.

Preface

This short study of the last phase of the medieval church in England argues the case that pre-Reformation religion was neither moribund nor oppressive, that ecclesiastical institutions were not in general corrupt or anachronistic, and that the majority of the clergy at every level struggled manfully to discharge the duties committed to their order. It is certain that the early Tudor church was in need of reform, as the church in all ages and in every location is in constant need of renewal in order to make it correspond more nearly, yet always imperfectly, to the divine model, which is itself a constantly shifting vision, reinterpreted generation by generation. That in the early sixteenth century the English church was subject to fierce criticism from within may be seen as a symptom of health rather than of terminal disease. The poor image which prevails in the popular mind today is in large measure the result of 'reading history backwards' – because the Reformation happened in England, it *must* have been necessary – and disproportionate attention has been devoted to any cases of 'scandal' or 'abuse' that have been found. Examination of surviving evidence, however, suggests that the vast majority of the English people were at least passively satisfied with the manner in which their church fulfilled both its religious and its social role.

It is perhaps difficult in this secular age to appreciate the extent to which historical interpretation of the Reformation era has been influenced until very recently by the legacy of confessional strife. It is not merely that Protestantism became identified with English nationalism, and papalism with the threat of foreign domination. Catholic historians, writing until the early 1960s in the shadow of the Council of Trent, sought to explain the necessity for and the success of the continental Counter-Reformation by the admission that the Latin church had in the later Middle Ages fallen away from the spiritual heights of the twelfth and thirteenth centuries, the age of SS Bernard of Clairvaux, Francis of Assisi and Thomas Aquinas, and that grace was restored only in the sixteenth century through the efforts of such giants as SS Ignatius Loyola and Charles Borromeo. The period from the early fourteenth to the early sixteenth centuries was conventionally seen as the ebb between two high tides of vigorous reforming activity, and in the absence of any obviously heroic figures, the great increase in active participation by a multitude of devout laypeople was obscured. In England, moreover, analysis of late medieval religion and ecclesiastical politics was retarded by an historiographical quirk – that the interests of medievalists tended to end in 1399, and those of early modern historians to start in the 1530s, with a brief nod backwards to 1471 or 1485. The fifteenth century has for many years now ceased to be the most neglected in English history, but old attitudes die hard.

It is hoped that the argument of the present study is solidly grounded in the many valuable works of research accomplished in recent years by late medieval and Tudor historians, both in the editing of those texts on which judgements must ultimately be based, and in studies of particular themes, dioceses and individuals. The selection of examples is inevitably influenced by the pattern of scholarship; thus, for instance, the diocese of Lincoln figures largely, both because of its vast geographical extent and because much excellent work has been published as the result of the study of its voluminous archives. Much illustrative material is also drawn from the diocese of Norwich, because in the late Middle Ages East Anglia was not a rural backwater, but one of the most prosperous and densely populated areas of England. I have attempted to concentrate on and to provide examples from the period 1471–1529, but it is impossible to explain the nature of early Tudor religion without frequent reference back to the later fourteenth century – a period which, it becomes increasingly clear, was of extraordinary significance in the history of the English church.

My infinite thanks are due to my colleagues in the teaching of Reformation history, Dr Sue Doran and Dr Chris Durston, who have constantly been prepared to discuss at length the matters treated here. They are in no way implicated in the views expressed, but their indefatigable help and encouragement is very much appreciated. Roger Lockyer most gently eliminated many verbal infelicities, and Professor Allen Brown greatly encouraged me at a moment of crisis. My greatest debt, as always, is to my wife, Dr Ruth Harvey, who read the book in draft and made very many constructive criticisms. To her this work is dedicated, with love and gratitude.

Christopher Harper-Bill

Part One: The Background

1 The Western Church in the Later Middle Ages

The late Middle Ages was a period of crisis, which is not to say that it was a time of decline. During the fourteenth century the buoyant confidence which had been the main characteristic of the expansionist western European society of the previous two hundred years was shattered by a concatenation of apparent disasters. The fall of Acre in 1291 marked the end of the crusader states on the mainland of Asia, and henceforth holy war was to be defensive, designed to stem Islamic incursions into Europe, but constantly hampered by the rivalries of western kings and princes. The flourishing economy of the thirteenth century, when land-hunger had resulted in the cultivation of the most marginal lands, suddenly collapsed with the deterioration of the climate, and Europe had suffered a series of appalling harvests and consequent famines in the second decade of the fourteenth century before her weakened population was for the first time in 1347 attacked by the plague known as the Black Death. In 1337 the simmering hostility between the kings of France and England erupted into open confrontation, and most other western powers were drawn into the endemic conflict which has become known as the Hundred Years War. The coincidence of warfare and pestilence which swept the Continent would have been enough to dispel the theological optimism of the central Middle Ages without a simultaneous crisis of authority within the church.

The arrest at Anagni in 1303 of Pope Boniface VIII by the agents of the king of France has long been regarded as a watershed in the history of the Catholic church, a reversal of that papal domination of western European religion established during the great reform movement of the late eleventh century and associated with Pope Gregory VII (1073–85). Many kings, including those of England, had in the twelfth and thirteenth centuries been able, in practice, to limit papal authority within their territories. Anagni is symptomatic, therefore, not so much of a recovery of real power over the church by the western monarchies, as of a fundamental shift of attitudes. In the late eleventh century secular rulers had

1

been stripped of their ritual functions as king-priests, the religious leaders of their people, and they had responded by developing bureaucratic forms of government which compensated for their loss of theocratic authority (**85**). The recovery and reception in the thirteenth century, through contact with Islam, of the political thought of the ancient Greek philosopher Aristotle led to the questioning of the papal assertion that the secular power had been established merely as a remedy for evil, necessary because of man's sinful nature and therefore reluctantly tolerated by God. An alternative view was now proposed, that the state was the result of man's natural tendency towards association, which was positively approved by God. The king was rehabilitated: no longer was power even in theory mediated to him by the pope, but rather it was granted to him by the voice of the people, which was equated with the voice of God. When Boniface VIII clashed with King Philip IV over the royal right to tax and exercise jurisdiction over the clergy of France, he was confronted not only by superior physical force, which was the perennial problem of the Papacy, but by an independently-based ideology of the state which owed nothing to papal interpretation of the Bible. Henceforth the king of France acted as religious leader of his people with little reference to the pope. The English king, more limited in his initiatives because of the effective balance of political power between crown, aristocracy, and the gentry and merchant classes represented in the emergent House of Commons, quietly tightened his control over the resources of the church within his realm, excusing himself to the pope by pleading the anti-papalism of Parliament which, despite his devotion to the Holy See, he was allegedly incapable of restraining (**76**).

In 1309 Pope Clement V established the Papacy at Avignon, in territory long held by the bishops of Rome. In view of the chronic disorder of the papal states in central Italy, this was a sensible move. From Avignon was financed a long and ultimately successful campaign to reduce the patrimony of St Peter around Rome to obedience and order. The machinery of ecclesiastical government did not collapse, rather its efficiency was enhanced; but the increasing sophistication displayed in the extraction from the western church of that money essential for the financing of central Italian campaigns caused the alienation of those whose purses were lightened by papal taxation. Also antagonised were those who experienced the erosion of their own resources of patronage at the hands of popes who, desperate to provide for their servants and to win support, expanded to the limits their plenitude of power in reserving to themselves appointment to an ever-extended range of lucrative ecclesiastical positions. This resentment was especially pronounced in England, where it was believed that the popes were the creatures of the enemy, the French king. English hostility was officially expressed in the passing by Parliament of the Statute of Provisors (1351), which forbade petitioning for or acceptance of papal appointment to ecclesiastical benefices (although this prohibition was ignored by the crown when papal initiative was to the advantage of royal servants), and the Statute of Praemunire (1353), which prohibited appeals to the papal court in any matter which might be interpreted as pertaining to royal jurisdiction. The spiritual authority of the Papacy was not in any way attacked: there was no challenge to its position as supreme arbiter in matters of faith, doctrine and religious practice. The church, however, was rooted in the land; it had been endowed by kings, lords and communities for the spiritual welfare of the people. Because the church had enormous economic assets and individual churches were held in English law to be pieces of real estate, the property and patronage rights of the English people, and most particularly of the king, must be safeguarded (**23, 76**). Since papal bureaucrats, operating according to the canon law of the church, in fact shared this view of churches as property, king and pope operated according to the same premises, and if their relationship was punctuated by clashes over the delineation of their respective rights, normality was a process of mutual accommodation.

English lamentation over the 'Babylonian Captivity' of the Papacy at Avignon was prompted by nationalistic and financial motives. A major crisis of spiritual authority was occasioned by the outbreak in 1378 of the Great Schism (**70**). Almost immediately after the return of the papal court to Rome, a group of French cardinals challenged the validity of the election of the Italian Pope Urban VI, and themselves elected one of their number as Pope Clement VII. A schism in the Papacy was not unprecedented: for periods amounting to fifty years during the twelfth century there had been rival claimants to the throne of St Peter, but it had usually been reasonably certain which one was the rightful pontiff and which one the creature of the German emperor, who was seeking to impose his own authority on central Italy. Now there was no such certainty. The situation was considerably aggravated by the political divisions of western Europe: since France and her allies recognised Clement VII and his successors who resettled at

Avignon, so those powers which were allied to England acknowledged the Roman line. Secular governments and great ecclesiastical bodies were, at a price, able to extract numerous concessions from the rival popes, each of whom was desperate to retain the loyalty of his supporters and whose spiritual revenues had been halved by the division of western Christendom into two obediences. This is not to say that the Schism was welcomed and cynically exploited. Throughout western Europe there was profound malaise, for it was an obvious scandal that the seamless robe of Christ which was the church should thus be rent apart. Universities, cathedral chapters and even secular governments devoted much agonised thought and effort to the resolution of the crisis, which prompted the fundamental question: where did ultimate authority within the church reside – in the pope, or in the college of cardinals who elected him, or in the whole body of bishops, or within the Christian community at large, acting through its representatives? There gradually emerged a consensus that only a general council of the church could resolve this impasse, and thus was inaugurated the period in the church's history known as the Conciliar Movement. According to the law of the church, however, only the pope could summon a general council. When the cardinals of both obediences at last seized the initiative and convened a council at Pisa in 1409, the outcome was not the resolution of the Schism, for neither pope accepted his deposition, but rather the creation of a third line of rival popes inaugurated by the election by the disillusioned cardinals of Pope Alexander V.

This chaos was resolved by the intervention of the Emperor Sigismund, who enjoyed far greater prestige and wielded more power than his immediate predecessors. He convened another general council at Constance in 1414 which, after the removal of the contending popes, three years later re-established an undivided Papacy by the election of Martin V. In this council the English delegates exercised a disproportionate influence, because of Henry V's spectacular military successes in France, and it was they who, operating under royal direction, ensured that a new and undisputed pope should be elected before any reforms were implemented. The reward for this was the English Concordat of 1418, by which Martin V formally conceded to the king the authority over the church in his realm which his predecessors had in fact enjoyed throughout the past century, and which was scarcely diminished by the pope's subsequent attempts to recover some measure of control over English ecclesiastical appointments.

The Council of Constance had proclaimed the overriding authority within the church of general councils, which should be held frequently. The Restoration Papacy was determined to reassert its own untrammelled position within the church. The two opposing theories of ecclesiastical government were brought into open conflict when the Council of Basle, summoned reluctantly in 1431, was almost immediately dissolved by Pope Eugenius IV but remained in session, ultimately initiating another potential schism by the election of its own 'pope'. The kings of western Europe, however, alarmed that rejection of the monarchical authority of the pope within the church might create a precedent for the restriction of their own powers, threw in their lot with the Papacy. The Council of Basle continued to meet until 1449, but it had long since become an irrelevance. The papal attitude to conciliarism is summarised by the decree of Pope Pius II in 1460, in which he stated that it was execrable to believe in the superiority of council over pope.

The popes of the Renaissance did not abdicate their spiritual responsibilities. They continued to legislate for the Christian commonwealth; they strove to organise the crusade so desperately needed for the defence of western Christendom after the fall of Constantinople to the Turks in 1453; and they built anew in the latest style to the greater glory of God. They were, however, constantly bedevilled by two horrific spectres – that the resurrection of conciliarism would jeopardise their spiritual authority, limited as that was in practice after the concordats with the various nations; and that the incursions of the Great Powers into Italy would destroy the autonomy of the papal states and reduce the pope to the role of domestic chaplain to the secular master of the peninsula, constrained by temporal domination to abandon his universal functions in favour of partisan action. Popes such as Alexander VI (1492–1503) and Julius II (1503–13) were violently criticised by contemporary writers for conduct far removed from the apostolic ideal; yet in the light of fifteenth-century developments their determination to maximise their power in central Italy, which was the keynote of their pontificates, was a rational and expedient policy. The use of Machiavellian strategies by the ruler of Rome was essential if the independence of the Vicar of Christ was to be maintained. The fusion of the two threats to the Papacy came with the summoning by the French king of a general council of the church at Pisa in 1511; the motivation was overtly political, and he received little support outside his own dominions. The Fifth

5

Lateran Council, which met from 1512 to 1517, was convened by the pope as a riposte to King Louis XII's initiative, but it was also the scene of profoundly serious discussion of the general reform of the church. Little was achieved, largely because the pope was haunted by the prospect of the diminution of his plenitude of power, and that little was also circumscribed by the vested interests of his own bureaucrats. Pope Leo X's experience of the council was such that he did not see fit to convene another assembly to meet the challenge of Martin Luther.

In the absence of papal support in the later Middle Ages for the numerous initiatives for a general reform of the church 'in head and members', there were many localised campaigns for spiritual regeneration. In the Low Countries and the Rhineland there emerged in the late fourteenth century a movement which became known as the *Devotio Moderna* (the modern devotion), whose key text was the significantly entitled *The Imitation of Christ*, by Thomas à Kempis. The adherents of the movement – men and women who, despite the suspicions of some contemporary ecclesiastics, remained strictly within the bounds of orthodoxy – attempted to live a common life based on the model of the monastic piety of the twelfth century, yet unrestrained by religious vows. The only evidence for such communities in England – where they were short-lived – comes from Norwich (**88**), but the ethos of intense meditation and strict morality was imported and fused with the native tradition of disciplined mysticism to influence the devotional lives of numerous literate English households. There was a continent-wide revival of strict forms of regular* life, characterised by the expansion of the Carthusian Order, the most austere of the traditional forms of the enclosed life; by the foundation of new orders such as the Bridgettines (established in 1378); and by the reform of many of the old orders by the institution of Observant wings, which adhered rigidly to the letter of their Rules and rejected the alleged laxity of modern times. The English province of the Carthusian Order was probably the most vigorous in Europe, and the Bridgettine house at Syon by the Thames was a centre of English spirituality; but of the Observant branches only that of the Franciscans was introduced into the kingdom in the late fifteenth century. The contribution of humanist scholars to reform, which consisted mainly of the establishment of authentic and purified texts and the criticism, more or less good-humoured, of so-called superstitious accretions to religion, had little effect on the beliefs or practice of the generality of Christians, but these inno vatory scholars were influential in the court circles of western Europe, and certainly in that of England in the early sixteenth century (**63**). The greatest of the Christian humanists, Desiderius Erasmus, who like most of his fellows remained an orthodox if discriminating Catholic, found hospitality in England and established a wide circle of friends and correspondents there.

The most effective reform, however, was that implemented on a national basis. By the early sixteenth century, although the spiritual unity of western Europe had been marred only by the existence of the separatist Hussite church in Bohemia, the organisation of the Latin church had become fragmented, so that the period from 1449 to 1517 has been characterised as 'the era of national churches' (**70**). Control of ecclesiastical finances and the selection of senior personnel was increasingly the prerogative of kings and other secular powers. What could be accomplished was demonstrated by the wide-ranging reforms achieved in the Spanish church by Cardinal Ximenez, who presided over it from 1495 to 1517 by the will of the pious queen, Isabella of Castille. He created an ambience in which humanist scholarship and intense mystical piety could flourish within the environment of fiercely orthodox religion and monarchical authoritarianism.

Such royal initiative for religious reform had been shown in England by King Henry V (1413–22), who was as eager to increase the effectiveness of the militia of Christ within his kingdom as he was to promote that of his temporal armies on the battlefields of France (**110**). The impetus was lost with his tragically premature death. Henry VI shared his father's intense piety, but his long minority, followed by his bouts of imbecility, resulted in his loss of control of the crown's extensive patronage, that most essential tool of government, and the quality of episcopal appointments temporarily declined as the leaders of factions around the court installed their own nominees. However, the vicissitudes of the English monarchy between 1399 and 1485 and the unfortunate involvement of ecclesiastics in the internecine strife which characterised Henry VI's reign do not appear to have resulted in a breakdown of clerical discipline or a crisis of faith. Financial investment in the church continued unabated in the middle years of the fifteenth century, and the laity continued to resort voluntarily to the church courts for the resolution of their disputes. When strong royal control of the church was reimposed by Edward IV (1461–83) and Henry VII (1485–1509), the able bishops whom they appointed were set at the head of a church which was, in its fundamental aspects, a healthy organism. There were, indeed, constant impassioned pleas for reform in England as on the Continent, but these should not be accepted uncritically as an indictment. They may be seen, rather, as a reflection of rising demands and expectations of performance which were clothed in conventional rhetoric, and as a sign of the vigour of the Roman church in its provinces which survived the crisis of authority at the centre.

Part Two: Analysis

2 The English Church, the Crown and the Papacy

Royal power

The firm control exercised by the crown over the church in England on the eve of the Reformation was no novelty, and until Henry VIII broke with Rome, the Tudor monarchs acted in accordance with long-established custom. From before the Norman Conquest English kings had shown an intense and obtrusive interest in the personnel, the finances and the spiritual efficacy of the church within their realm. The vigorous assertion by the Papacy and its advocates in the late eleventh century of the supreme authority of Rome within a western European church in which national frontiers were merely convenient divisions of a unified Christian commonwealth had done little, in the long term, to diminish royal power. Papal competence in matters of doctrine and moral jurisdiction was recognised, but even in the aftermath of the confrontation between Henry II and Thomas Becket those rights which were most profitable or useful to the king were little diminished. The Papacy might threaten to depose rulers who contravened its interpretation of the plan for the government of Christian society outlined by God in the Bible, but it was only when kings were thought by their own subjects to have flouted social and constitutional conventions that papal declaration of the divine law might threaten the position of a ruler who had already sacrificed the support of his vassals. The decline of papal prestige in the later Middle Ages lessened even this constraint (**36, 85**).

The long papal residence at Avignon and the assumption, general if incorrect, that the pope was the creature of the king of France fostered a nationalistic view of the English church. From the reign of Edward I prayers and processions for the success of the king in war had regularly been staged throughout the realm. Such liturgical propaganda became more frequent from the outbreak of the Hundred Years War. By the 1350s a popular verse held that the pope had become French, but Jesus had become

English. The Chancellor in the Parliament of 1377, when the future Richard II was adopted as heir to the throne, opined that God had demonstrated by giving victory to the English that they were now His chosen people, as the Israelites once had been, and that He had now sent Prince Richard for their redemption, as He had previously sent His own son (**76, 160, 184**). This potential saviour was deposed in 1399 and subsequently murdered, but despite the unfortunate English habit of killing their kings (regarded by the French as a prime indication of their barbarism), the secular ruler was presented as leader of the church in terms which had not been used since the successful papal demolition of the religious image of kingship in the late eleventh century. The revival of theocratic kingship was facilitated by the scandal of the papal Schism, during which the king took all the vital decisions which affected the English church (**59**). One early fifteenth-century preacher described Henry V as the celestial warrior sent to smite heretics at home and Frenchmen abroad – 'he is the column which supports the whole temple'. The church was seen as a national institution, part of the realm; the Papacy was not attacked, it was merely peripheral. That these views reflected official attitudes is clearly demonstrated by the leadership given by the victor of Agincourt to the English church in matters of reform and even of liturgy (**110, 135**).

The rhetoric of royal authority sounded rather hollow during the adult years of Henry VI, a child of whom so much had been hoped but whose reign, despite his undoubted personal piety, witnessed the nadir of English monarchy. Paradoxically, however, that febrile king's reputation was transformed after 1485 by his Tudor successor, who quite inappropriately fostered a cult of Henry VI as an exemplar of Christian kingship, the antithesis of the evil Yorkist usurper Richard III. If Henry VII repaired the financial fortunes of the crown by the unlovable techniques of the counting-house, it has been convincingly argued that he restored the status of kingship by the creation of a vibrant political theology (**130**). This was surely, however, no innovation based on continental *exempla*, but a revival of the claims to ecclesiastical authority exercised by Henry V, who, it has been asserted, 'in all but name' acted as 'supreme governor of the Church of (*sic*) England' (**110,** p. 115).

The use of the translation 'Church of England' (rather than 'Church in England') for the Latin *ecclesia Anglicana* is controversial, for it implies an existence separate and distinct from the Latin western church under the pope. It is certainly true that the universal church was seen as consisting of a number of singular churches constituted on a national basis, and fifteenth-century archbishops of Canterbury referred in official pronouncements to the excellence above others of the English church (**141**). Yet it is important to emphasise that, until Henry VIII's matrimonial crisis, the supreme authority of the pope in spiritual and doctrinal matters was challenged only by the Lollard heretics. The English church was, however, subject to two laws – the canon law of western Christendom, based largely on papal rulings, and the common law of England. The church was both a spiritual and a temporal institution: it existed within the realm; the church building was regarded as a piece of real estate; and prelates held their estates of the king by the same tenure as lay lords. The church was both subject to and protected by the laws of England. Problems arose in that ill-defined borderland of issues which might, with some justification, be claimed for either jurisdiction. For example, did definition of benefit of clergy (which conferred immunity from secular justice in criminal cases) pertain to the ecclesiastical authorities culminating in the pope, or to the king in Parliament as the embodiment of the common law of England, from which exemption was granted? This question had been at the heart of the Becket controversy in the 1160s; when it was resurrected in 1515, the legal debate ended with Wolsey on behalf of the English clergy begging the king's pardon and with the vigorous assertion by Henry VIII that 'kings in England in past time have never had any superior but God alone' (**43**, p. 166). This statement and previous decisions by English judges, maintaining that royal action within the limits of the common law should override papal mandates, were certainly taken by the king during the crisis of the breach with Rome as precedents for the total rejection of papal authority, but the context was entirely different. The royal judges, and Henry VIII himself in 1515, were reasserting in vigorous terms the claim effectively advanced by English kings since the Conquest to monitor the reception of canon law in their realm and to reject those elements which ran counter to the customary law of the kingdom or derogated from their own royal dignity. Neither common law, royal decree nor Parliamentary statute had attempted to regulate the faith of Englishmen, save only by the proscription of heresy, against which the Papacy had consistently urged that the civil power should take measures.

The outcome of the crisis over benefit of clergy in 1515 was that, although the clergy sued for royal pardon, the controversial statute depriving those in minor orders of benefit in cases of murder and robbery was not renewed (**56**). This conclusion epitomises the spirit of compromise which was usual in jurisdictional matters. *Causes célèbres*, in the early sixteenth century as in the twelfth, distract attention from that co-operation between the secular power and the ecclesiastical authorities which was the norm. Thus the Papacy in 1487 at the request of the English government reiterated the canonical rules for the conduct of those who sought sanctuary and authorised the crown to appoint custodians to prevent malefactors leaving such places. Henry VII, however, claimed the right to remove from sanctuary those charged with high treason, and emphasised that it was the peculiar nature of this crime, rather than any desire to undermine ecclesiastical immunity, which prompted this action; there was no serious threat to abolish sanctuary until 1540 (**149**). Notwithstanding the Statute of Praemunire, which forbade judicial appeals outside the realm, cases were permitted to go to the court of Rome provided that royal interests were not at stake; thus Cardinal Morton, despite his influence, was twice challenged before papal judges by those who resisted his alleged extension of the authority of the archbishop of Canterbury (**138**). In 1499 the episcopal right to report excommunicates to Chancery, so that royal officers would attempt their capture, was extended to papal judges-delegate, who had never enjoyed it before (**61**). Despite the availability from Chancery of a writ of prohibition, which in a specific case ordered termination of proceedings in a church court, those tribunals were still in the late fifteenth century able to maintain their canon-law jurisdiction in many areas which were in theory, according to the common law, beyond their competence. The crown was content to allow this, so long as the king's own interests were not threatened (**145**).

Royal support for the maintenance of ecclesiastical liberties was certainly not absolute. In response to yet another round of the perennial complaints from the representatives of the clergy about breaches of their immunity, Edward IV in 1462 granted them a charter forbidding all common-law prosecutions of clerks in holy orders, or the use of the Statute of Praemunire (intended to impede unauthorised cases at Rome) against judges and litigants in English church courts. The charter was confirmed by Richard III in 1484, yet neither king thought it worth their while to steer through Parliament a statute to this effect, which would have given far greater protection, perhaps for fear of alienating the considerable number of common lawyers in the lower house, traditionally jealous of the comprehensive jurisdiction of the courts in which they practised (**9, 40**). It has been strongly argued that the position of the church was weakened by the laicisation of the personnel of government and by the rise of the gentleman civil-servant (**37**). The chancellorship, however, was continually held by a prelate from 1455 to 1529 and the keeper of the privy seal was invariably an ecclesiastic. Lawyers of the archbishop's Court of Canterbury, moreover, were consistently employed in royal service. Certainly there were those in the inner circle of royal government who sought to undermine ecclesiastical jurisdiction, such as Sir James Hobart, Attorney-General to Henry VII, who encouraged actions of Praemunire (**86**). Most of these date from that king's last years, a period notable for the policy of fiscal terrorism adopted by the government, and the primary motive behind these prosecutions was probably to extract lucrative fines in return for the king's forgiveness. Yet the period of Wolsey's ascendency has been seen by one historian of the church courts as a time of recovery after the attacks upon them and the demoralisation which followed Morton's death (**49**). The latitude allowed to ecclesiastical judges might vary according to shifts in the balance of power within the king's council and the dictates of expediency, but it was only after 1529 that a concerted attack was mounted. Measures taken thereafter were not the inevitable culmination of a programme pursued consistently by the government since 1485, for early Tudor policy towards the church had many twelfth-century and thirteenth-century precedents, and no king of that earlier period would have contemplated a breach with Rome.

In two important respects, however, royal control of the English church was consistently and ruthlessly implemented. A government constantly desperate for money imposed an increasingly heavy burden of taxation on the clergy. From the late fourteenth century the Convocations of Canterbury and York, provincial councils which had originated as assemblies for the implementation of reform, began to be summoned regularly at the time of Parliament at the instance of the king. Discussion of, and eventual acquiescence in, royal demands for taxation dominated these meetings of the clergy (**54**). Between 1401 and 1496 the northern Convocation voted thirty clerical subsidies, and the far richer province of Canterbury made forty-seven grants to the crown. The average annual contribution of the church to royal finances by this means alone was at least £7600 per annum, and between 1485 and 1534

13

this rose to £9000 a year (the decrease in real terms because of inflation was made good in other ways). Although some justification was always attempted in terms of danger to the realm, clerical taxation from the early fifteenth century onwards was not confined to wartime emergencies; the royal demands were becoming predictable, but none the less burdensome for that (**40, 173**) [**doc. 2a**]. The net, moreover, was tightened to include those churches which had been exempted in the great survey of ecclesiastical wealth of 1291 and whose income had since increased, and also the unbeneficed clergy, who were forced to pay a 'charitable subsidy' to the archbishop, which was granted by him to the crown (**119**). In addition to this regular taxation the crown took the temporal revenues of vacant bishoprics and abbeys and then demanded a fine for restitution of these to the new incumbent, while individual well-to-do ecclesiastics came under increasing pressure to grant 'benevolences' to the king. The English church was richly endowed, but the government, with ever-increasing determination and efficiency, ensured that it contributed handsomely to the common good of king and people.

The crown also made full use of its rights of patronage, not only to determine the composition of the hierarchy of the church but also to reward its servants at minimal cost to itself. It has been suggested that the king's ecclesiastical patronage became less important as more and more laymen were employed in governmental service (**37**), but a glance at the composition of cathedral chapters* in the early sixteenth century indicates that the government had not loosened its hold on their rich prebends, and every episcopal register reveals the continued exercise of its rights in favour of royal servants seeking richer parochial livings. Bishops, who were themselves royal nominees, were susceptible to pressure even when the king did not hold the right of presentation. If in fact there were fewer king's clerks to be rewarded, those who remained were highly acquisitive, while any surplus patronage could be utilised to build up a less formal royal clientele. It has been demonstrated how in the fourteenth century the king's judges in such matters 'raised royal interest into an impregnable legal doctrine' (**112**, p. 297). In the case of disputed advowsons* to which the king had a claim, however tenuous, the rights in canon law of diocesan bishops and the occupants of benefices were swept aside. Patronage was a crucial aspect of finance, and the financial control of the English church by the crown was absolute.

Papal authority and influence

The popes of the Renaissance were determined to exercise the plenitude of power enjoyed by their predecessors before the Great Schism and the consequent upsurge of conciliar theory. To counter the pernicious doctrine that a general council of the church was superior to the pope, they were prepared to make wide-ranging concessions to the kings and princes of western Europe in order to win their support. In the English Concordat of 1418 Pope Martin V, in recognition of Henry V's crucial role at the Council of Constance, which had resulted in the restoration of almost untrammelled papal monarchy (in theory at least), and in return for continuing support against the pretensions of a future general council, granted to the king that authority over the church in England which in effect he already enjoyed. That these concessions were greater than those made to any other European ruler is a measure of the tight internal control already exercised by the English crown and of the temporary domination by Henry V of the international diplomatic situation (**52, 70**).

This was followed by a period of readjustment. In the 1420s Martin V conducted a concerted campaign to achieve the repeal of the Statute of Provisors, which almost totally restricted his freedom to appoint to lucrative ecclesiastical offices in England, and which he regarded as an unwarranted diminution of papal power. The English government was intensely suspicious of Roman attempts to undermine the customs of the realm, and Archbishop Chichele was ground between two mill-stones (**52, 59**). The Papacy eventually appreciated, however, that even in the faction-ridden England of Henry VI it had no hope of implementing its claim to universal authority in those matters where the interests of the crown were at stake. When the Council of Basle set itself up in opposition to the pontiff and renewed the schism by electing an 'anti-pope', the papal legate in England did everything possible to highlight the danger to all secular rulers of an assault upon the papal monarchy, and Eugenius IV, otherwise an intransigent pope, was prepared to ratify all previous concessions in order to win English support. In this he succeeded. Although in 1511 Pope Julius II at last convened another general council (the Fifth Lateran) at Rome, he did so merely in response to the schismatic council convened for political reasons at Pisa by the king of France, who wished to embarrass the pope. There was much sincere talk of reform, but little was achieved. The English delegation to the papal council was tiny, and little interest seems to have been taken in its proceedings (**52, 93**).

The Restoration Papacy was increasingly enmeshed in the politics of the Italian peninsula. It would be wrong to regard this as a sinister trend, the abdication of universal spiritual responsibilities for the sake of the ambitions of a territorial prince. Then, as always, if the Papacy was to remain at the head of an independent institution which transcended national boundaries, it was essential that it should not fall under the domination of any one monarch or nation, to whose interests its moral authority would be annexed. The re-establishment of papal power in central Italy in the early fifteenth century was, however, an expensive business, and as the major European states became increasingly committed in the peninsula – which after the French invasion of 1494 became a battleground of foreign armies – the Papacy, in order to preserve its autonomy, had to commit itself to constantly increasing expenditure and to resort to tortuous diplomatic expedients.

One obvious consequence of the complex international situation was that the Papacy became ever more amenable to the wishes of the English crown, for whose support Rome was often desperate. It was not merely that Henry VII and his son were granted conventional marks of papal favour, such as the despatch to them of the honorific cap and sword of maintenance. After some initial hesitation and delay in acceding to his wishes, once the first Tudor appeared to be securely established on the throne and England had re-emerged as an international power, the popes reverted to their former policy of accommodation, designed now to win political rather than ideological support. The cardinal protectors of England, salaried by the king, and the resident ambassadors in Rome, were primarily occupied in diplomatic negotiations, but they also served the ecclesiastical interests of the king and his subjects, petitioning on their behalf for appointments, dispensations and indulgences. Not only did the king obtain provision of all his own candidates to English, and also to Irish, sees, but this was achieved on his own terms, most spectacularly in the case of the bishopric of Durham. Left vacant for five years during which the crown took its extensive revenues, it was filled in 1507 by the provision of Christopher Bainbridge, English ambassador at Rome, on condition that for seven years a substantial portion of its income should be diverted to the repair of England's northern defences. Within a year Bainbridge was translated to York, the king's secretary

Thomas Ruthall was appointed to Durham, and the diversion of revenues was now extended in time to eight years and in scope to include the construction of new military installations. The pope complained of the unprecedented nature of these concessions, but in the end capitulated to royal demands. This is indicative of the lengths to which the Papacy would go to secure guaranteed English support (**62, 93**).

There was very little for which the English government asked which was not given. Bishops were translated from see to see at Henry VII's whim in order that faithful servants might receive an increasing scale of rewards and the crown might profit from the vacancies. Because of the English loss of Normandy, ecclesiastical jurisdiction over the Channel Islands was transferred from the Norman diocese of Coutances to Winchester, and after Henry VIII's capture of Tournai, that diocese was temporarily annexed to Wolsey's York. A dispensation was granted for Prince Henry's marriage to his brother's widow, and after he became king Henry was permitted to annex monastic property to enrich his father's collegiate foundations. Indulgences were freely granted to those churches favoured by the royal family, and king's clerks received numerous dispensations for pluralism, which would increase their income at no cost to the crown (**59, 62, 93**). The late medieval kings of England, especially the Tudors, received most, if not all, they asked of the Papacy. The very fact that so much had been given worsened the shock of rejection when, because of changed political circumstances in Italy, Pope Clement VII, who had himself been cardinal protector of England, was unable to expedite the annulment of Henry VIII's first marriage.

Since the early thirteenth century the Papacy had sought to tax the English clergy, like those of other provinces, to provide for the urgent necessities of the Roman church. The crown had always diverted to itself a large proportion of this revenue, in return for allowing the papal collectors to operate in England, while the Papacy had incurred all the resentment for the imposition. In the fifteenth century, however, papal requests for taxation met with little response, for the crown was able to tap clerical resources itself. Polite excuses were the order of the day. A particularly good example of English attitudes is provided by Alexander VI's demand for a subsidy for the protection of Christendom against the Turks. Henry VII, following the example of Edward IV in 1464, and pleading the liberties of the church and realm of England, persuaded the pope to exempt England from the tax, but told the clergy that it was right that a grant should be made to the crown which might be used for the war against Islam. Both Yorkist and Tudor kings claimed that by placing themselves between pope and clergy they were protecting the English church (**54, 59, 62**).

It was, however, the king rather than the pope whose financial exactions were to be feared. It has been calculated that between 1485 and the break with Rome, the total amount rendered by the English church to Rome in Peter's Pence*, in the fees paid by certain religious houses for their privileges, in the procurations* of the papal collector and in fees connected with appointment to benefices, amounted to an annual average of £4816. In the same period the crown, in taxation and occasional revenues, was taking on average £12,500 a year from the church, in addition to the revenues of vacant bishoprics and abbeys, loans, and 'benevolences' extracted from individuals. The first two Tudors were, in fact, receiving from the church more than two-and-a-half times the sum conveyed to the court of Rome (**173**).

The difficulty of obtaining direct taxation, combined with rising military and diplomatic expenses in central Italy and the financing of the projected crusade, placed an enormous strain upon the papal budget. In 1429 revenue had fallen to one third of the pre-Schism level, and although there was thereafter a marked rise in income from the papal states, this alone would not suffice. The papal curia was compelled to maximise its spiritual revenues. Fees rose for all services provided by the court and its officials, who increasingly had purchased their offices and naturally sought to make a profit from them. The canonisation of St Osmund of Salisbury in 1456 cost the enormous sum of £731 13s (£731 65p), and it was probably the estimated expense which deterred Henry VII from proceeding with the canonisation of his Lancastrian predecessor Henry VI, despite encouragement from Rome. While the cost of an indulgence offered directly to individuals was by no means extortionate, English corporations paid heavily for general pardons which they offered to their benefactors; in the early sixteenth century the guild of St Mary of Boston paid over £3200 for a plenary indulgence (**62**). Litigation at the court of Rome was also expensive, and this is probably why so few English cases are recorded in the *Rota*, the central tribunal of the papal court; only a prelate with the resources of Archbishop Morton of Canterbury could afford the costs of long legal battles there (**14**).

Most English people who came into contact with the papal curia did so when they sought some dispensation from the rules of canon law which could only be granted by the pope [**doc. 3**]. Clerks, for example, might petition for papal licence to hold in plurality two incompatible benefices; monks might seek to serve a parish church and to live outside the cloister; potential ordinands might beg exemption from the bar placed on their progress to the priesthood by their bastardy or by some physical deformity; laypeople might wish to marry although they were related within the wide spectrum of prohibited degrees. Other dispensations commonly sought were permission to have a portable altar, so that Mass might be celebrated in private; or for absolution from some vow rashly undertaken. Such dispensations are by far the largest category of English business recorded in the papal registers of the late fifteenth century, and it has been remarked that papal authority with regard to the English church was mainly the authority to dispense. A papal clerk in 1474 noted tartly that a petitioner for plurality need not have been so scrupulous and pedantic in his statement; he would have obtained his request in any case, especially because he was an Englishman and the pope had been more liberal in grants to the English than to any other nation [**doc. 3a**]. Seeking a dispensation for his marriage in 1473, William Paston noted that a proctor at Rome had told him that the pope did this many times every day (**40**). The English entries in the registers of Pope Sixtus IV (1471–84) indeed reveal that there was constant recourse to the court of Rome for a wide variety of indults* and dispensations, and that the petitioners ranged from the royal family and courtiers in search of various spiritual privileges to the inhabitants of Rotsea (Yorkshire) seeking permission for a chapel because of the inaccessibility of their parish church, and to a priest devastated because he had accidentally killed a boy while practising archery (**7**).

Full analysis of the early sixteenth-century situation is not possible until publication of the concluding volumes of the *Calendar of Papal Registers*, but from the evidence of printed bishops' registers there is no indication of any great lessening of contact. In the diocese of Bath and Wells twenty-four dispensations granted by Pope Julius II (1503–13) are noted, and Bishop Booth's Hereford register contains interesting examples issued by Pope Leo X (1513–21), whose pontificate was subsequently regarded by officials at Rome as a golden age, because of the great number of such documents which he authorised (**2, 22**).

Throughout the late Middle Ages the Papacy from time to time granted plenary indulgences*, remitting the penalties of sin for those making some contribution to causes in which it had a special interest. The multiplication of such pardons has been criticised as an 'inflationary spiral' (**85**, p. 133): frequent offers of remission, it is argued, devalued that divine grace which the Vicar of Christ might bestow upon the faithful from the 'treasury of merits' accumulated most especially by Christ (of which the extent was infinite), but also by the saints. It is certain, however, that English people were still eager to obtain these benefits. Most plenary indulgences which were preached in England after 1450 were granted in order to raise money for the defensive crusade in the eastern Mediterranean against the Ottoman Turks. It is estimated that in 1498–99 two thousand English priests obtained the indulgence for the relief of the burdens of the Roman church, which allowed them to grant plenary absolution to their parishioners; and the historian Polydore Vergil noted the great sums received by the pope for the prosecution of holy war from the Jubilee indulgence of 1500 (**62**) [**doc. 4b**].

Many English churches petitioned the pope for remission of punishment for pilgrims and benefactors. Normally these were partial indulgences, waiving a certain number of years of penance. All monarchs sought and obtained generous indulgences for their own foundations, Henry VI for Eton, Edward IV for St George's Chapel at Windsor, Henry VII for his chapel at Westminster and his hospital at the Savoy. Many lesser patrons and ecclesiastical corporations followed their example [**doc. 4a**], and it was not always stipulated that a financial contribution should be made: a nobleman, for example, might obtain such a grant in order to multiply prayers at the tombs of his ancestors. Both Henry VII and his heir prized highly the personal indulgences granted to them by the pope. Henry VIII obtained such on three occasions, and in 1525 Wolsey reported the king's delight at being informed that he might obtain the Jubilee indulgence for pilgrims to Rome by visiting three English churches. Numerous institutions with papal indulgences ordered the printing of letters of confraternity*, in which the name of the contributor could later be inserted; such bulk production itself illustrates their popularity (**62, 186**).

In view of the bad publicity which attended papal indulgences as a result of Luther's onslaught, it is worth emphasising that they normally served good causes on an international or a local scale – the defence of Christendom or the reconstruction of holy places struck by disaster. In 1529, during the crisis of the divorce, Henry VIII refused to allow the preaching of an indulgence in aid of the crusade, because by this means so much money had already been taken out of the kingdom; yet when the indulgence for St Peter's at Rome, which had sparked Luther's protest, was preached in England, the crown had taken one quarter of the profits in return for its acquiescence. There had been criticism of indulgences since the late fourteenth century, but apart from that of the Lollards, who denied papal authority, the attack was on abuses of the system rather than on the theological rationale. The bishops were eager to apprehend the purveyors of false pardons, who were simply confidence-tricksters; and countless orthodox preachers for generations before Erasmus had emphasised what popes and theologians had always stipulated, that no indulgence was effective without confession and true repentance for sins committed. On the very eve of the English Reformation, Christopher St German, legal apologist for the royal supremacy, abhorred alleged financial abuses precisely because he considered indulgences an essential part of the scheme of salvation. The vast majority of papal indulgences offered in England were, however, solicited by Englishmen or by native institutions, and were not a blatant exercise in papal fiscalism imposed upon an unwilling flock (**62, 83**).

Whereas the exercise of papal jurisdiction in England in the twelfth and thirteenth centuries has been extensively studied, little attention has been devoted to the operation of the system in the century before the Reformation. Yet despite the limitations imposed by the Statute of Praemunire, there were many matters of purely ecclesiastical import, where royal interests were not affected, in which the arbitration and judgement of the papal court and its local agents were still freely solicited. Between 1476 and 1478 the Abbot of Abingdon acted as legate* *a latere* in England, and in 1485 Pope Innocent VIII's legate granted the initial dispensation for Henry VII's marriage to Elizabeth of York (**87**). More regular were the activities of papal judges-delegate. A rough count reveals twenty-nine cases committed by the pope to English judges between 1471 and 1484, and it is quite certain that not all cases were recorded in the papal registers. The judges had to deal with a wide range of matters – matrimonial causes, election disputes in monasteries, and allegations of the misappropriation of tithes and bequests. During the pontificate of Pope Sixtus IV, English litigants were still utilising the highest ecclesiastical tribunal and native judges were accustomed to the receipt of judicial commissions from Rome (**7**).

There is much scattered evidence of continued papal judicial activity in the early sixteenth century. In 1512, for example, the bishops of the province of Canterbury appealed to Rome not only against the archbishop's probate jurisdiction, but also against the abuse of their privileges by the friars and Hospitallers (**1, 71**). In 1513 papal judges-delegate determined a dispute about the obligations of residence of clergy at St Paul's Cathedral; in 1517 a dispute between the monks of Coventry and their bishop was heard at Rome; and in the following year the Bishop of Hereford asked the pope to adjudicate upon the statutes of his cathedral church (**2, 93**). Most significantly, in 1518 the Court of Aldermen of London appealed to Rome for clarification of the arrangements for tithe payments in the city; laymen too were still utilising papal jurisdiction (**106**). It cannot be sufficiently emphasised that the initiative in activating papal judicial machinery, as in the search for indulgences and dispensations, came from the English 'consumers'. In the twelfth century papal justice had expanded because the papal court offered a superior judicial product, for the benefits of which clergy and laypeople all over western Europe had been prepared to pay. By 1500 the quality of local ecclesiastical jurisdiction had improved immeasurably, but there were still certain circumstances which could prompt Englishmen to appeal to Rome. The judicial and dispensing powers of the pope were only seriously called into question, other than by underground heretics, when the king found to his horror that international political circumstances had caused the 'well of grace' (**40**, p. 99) to run dry.

The spiritual authority of the Roman church was therefore universally accepted and its judicial competence was challenged only when the interests of the English government were at stake. It is infinitely more difficult to determine whether any great affection was felt for the Papacy. The main causes of earlier resentment had now been removed. Parliamentary legislation in the later fourteenth century had curtailed Roman inroads on English ecclesiastical patronage, and the clergy were no longer subject to escalating papal taxation as in the thirteenth and early fourteenth centuries. In thirty months in the years 1504 to 1507, 489 English visitors were recorded at the English hospice in Rome, and scattered wills make provision for a pilgrimage to the Holy City for the soul of the deceased. In 1475 Lord Rivers, brother-in-law of the king, journeyed to Rome for the Jubilee indulgence, which a man of his status could easily have obtained at home. Such expeditions, however, were probably prompted more by the desire to visit the tombs of the martyrs or by the instincts of the tourist than by devotion to the pope; indeed, in 1500 a Cistercian abbot complained that those monks who did not go to Rome as sinners returned as such (**7, 59, 139**).

Marks of honour bestowed by the Papacy were gladly accepted by the English royal house, culminating in the title 'Defender of the Faith', which placed the king on a par with his rival, 'the most Christian king' of France. News of Pope Julius II's election prompted a solemn celebration at St Paul's. There is very little evidence by the mid-fifteenth century of direct anti-papalism. The London cordwainers had in 1468 derided papal prohibition of their manufacture of ostentatiously pointed shoes, but easy circumvention of this ban by appeal to the crown probably calmed their emotions. More revealing than the scorn shown by one man towards the papal bull excommunicating rebels against Henry VII is the popular belief, sedulously fostered by the king, that the perpetrator of this outrage instantly dropped dead (**59, 87**). For most English people, from the royal court circle to the inhabitants of rural hamlets who might benefit from an indulgence obtained for a local church, the Papacy was part of the traditional order of things, as much in Yorkist and early Tudor England as three centuries before.

3   The English Bishops

The medieval bishop had a dual role, as father in God to the flock committed to his charge and as a great territorial lord. He held his pastoral office through unbroken apostolic succession from the original companions of Jesus. Jurisdiction was, in theory, granted to him by the pope, according to the doctrine that Christ had committed government of the church to St Peter, who had then delegated authority to the other apostles; for his lands he rendered homage to the king. The ideal bishop should be a repository of spiritual wisdom, but he was also expected to engage in that conspicuous expenditure, in building works and in hospitality, which was the mark of good lordship. He was responsible for the religious welfare of a multitude of souls, for there were only twenty-one dioceses in England and Wales, whereas there were over two hundred and fifty in contemporary Italy. The diocese of Norwich, for example, contained over thirteen hundred parishes. He supervised the management of extensive resources; the revenues of Winchester, the richest bishopric in western Christendom, amounted to the huge sum of £3880 per annum, and even St David's, poor by English standards, had an annual income of £457. Because of the enormous obligations which lay upon all bishops, however, even the richest of them was perennially indebted. A bishop was constantly on the move between his manor houses, often excluded from his own cathedral by a jealous chapter* and compelled by his responsibilities and by economic necessity to live in the saddle. Outside his own diocese he was obliged to attend Parliament, for he owed the service of counsel to the king, and also to go to the provincial assemblies convened by his archbishop. He was responsible for the collection of royal taxation from his clergy, and he might be despatched on vital diplomatic missions or set at the head of a department of state. He was also expected to be a learned man, ideally a scholar and a benefactor of education. The demands of episcopacy were extraordinarily heavy, and it is amazing how conscientiously they were discharged by the vast majority of medieval English bishops (**37, 45, 153**).

24

From before the Norman Conquest the crown had exercised firm control over the composition of the English episcopate. In the early twelfth century Henry I had conceded that there should be free election of bishops by their cathedral chapters, but by refusing homage for the lands of the see the king could still exercise an effective veto. The alleged writ of Henry II to the monks of Winchester in 1173 – 'I order you to hold a free election, nevertheless I forbid you to elect anyone save Richard Archdeacon of Poitiers, my clerk' – may be apocryphal, but it expresses the reality of effective royal selection. From the fourteenth century the papal claim to appoint directly to bishoprics was rejected in the parliamentary Statute of Provisors; the king himself was less dogmatic, but in practice papal freedom of action was almost totally curtailed (**76**). In all but exceptional cases, the king made his choice, the chapter elected the royal nominee and the pope provided him to his see [**doc. 2b**].

Critics of the system, in the early sixteenth century as in the twelfth, might inveigh against royal tyranny, but it is doubtful if any alternative system would have worked better. Free canonical election could not, in the real world, take place in a vacuum; local secular interests would intrude, and on those few occasions when freedom was allowed, a fiercely disputed election was a not uncommon consequence (**85**). The Papacy was far removed from England and for that reason susceptible to partial advice. The greatest of the medieval popes, Innocent III, at the moment when King John submitted to him as a vassal in 1214, spoke wisely when he instructed that bishops should be chosen who were loyal to the king and useful to the realm (**36**). The point is not that English kings would very occasionally advance manifestly holy men who were subsequently recognised as saints by the universal church, but that the majority of royal appointees who had made their way in the world as crown servants did turn out to be conscientious diocesan bishops. This was as true under Henry VII as under Henry II (**140**). It is arguable that modern historians, as much as medieval chroniclers, have been too much influenced by the dramatic example of Thomas Becket, and that scores of bishops over nearly four centuries who sought to implement ecclesiastical reform through co-operation with the crown have been much undervalued. The efficiency and endurance which had brought civil servants to the king's attention were the indispensable qualities of the hard-pressed prelates. The itinerant life of the active bishop was not dissimilar from that of the king's justices, and the task of both was the same, to create order according to the principles of the law.

It is often implied that the quality of the English episcopate declined in the later Middle Ages. There are two main reasons for this false impression. The first is that bishops were sharply criticised by contemporary satirists and moralisers, particularly in the extensive sermon literature of the period (**75, 84**). Many preachers were motivated by a strong desire for reform and renewal. They compared the church of their own times with the primitive community described in the Acts of the Apostles, found it sadly wanting, and not unnaturally laid much of the blame at the door of its leaders. Ardent reformers are not noted for judicious analysis, and these vociferous critics, who were usually free of any extensive pastoral responsibility, failed to appreciate that leadership of a church thoroughly integrated with secular society was a task very different from the inspiration of the persecuted Christian sect of the first three centuries. It is perhaps a measure of the maturity of late medieval Christianity that the concepts of reform promulgated by the bishops of the twelfth and thirteenth centuries had taken such deep root that the model of the ideal church could now be turned against the episcopal order. This groundswell of criticism, which bishops did little to stifle, is a symptom neither of the rise of heterodoxy nor of a decline in the quality of bishops, but rather of the desire to achieve, within the framework of the Catholic church, a form of episcopal perfection unattainable within a society which expected its ecclesiastical leaders to fulfil such a multitude of roles. When John Colet in his Convocation sermon of 1512 urged the need for bishops to amend their lives as a prelude to reformation of the church at large, he merely composed a new humanistic variation on a traditional theme, and his exhortation to action cannot be taken as a true bill of indictment, although it was eagerly seized upon by the early Protestants. It is notable, indeed, that Colet was invited to preach by an archbishop of Canterbury who, while serving as Chancellor of England, had six months earlier conducted an extensive personal visitation of his own diocese (**140**).

The second reason for the image of late medieval episcopal torpor is the difference between the categories of evidence available to historians of the twelfth and fifteenth centuries. The existence of a few invaluable collections of correspondence allows some twelfth-century bishops to emerge as personalities who responded spiritually and intellectually to the call for reform. No such collection exists for any fifteenth-century bishop. The late medieval historian has instead to contend with numerous bulky bishops' registers – the product, just like the endless parchment rolls produced by the royal administration, of that revolution in record-keeping which occurred around 1200. Documents produced by a bureaucratic machine reveal few traces of the personality of the man whom it serves. The late medieval bishops therefore appear as colourless figures, lacking in zeal and subservient to routine.

The creation of that routine, and of the machinery for its implementation, was in fact one of the greatest achievements of the medieval church. In the twelfth century the parameters of reforming action had been established: innumerable thorny problems relating to the discipline and religious observance of clergy, monks and laity had required individual solution, for there were few precedents. Bishops were constantly consulting the pope in order to establish the law (**36**). In the thirteenth century, on the basis of innumerable papal decisions in specific cases, a comprehensive set of rulings on every aspect of religious and ecclesiastical life was formulated in a universal code of canon law. In particular the decrees of the Fourth Lateran Council of 1215, supplemented for England by the statutes of the two papal legates Otto (1237–41) and Ottobuono (1265–68), created a framework of legislation which provided answers to most problems which would confront a bishop in his diocese. The late medieval bishops' registers, prolix and repetitive as they may sometimes seem, record the automatic implementation of the reform programme of an earlier age. They are a reflection of ever-increasing efficiency and professionalism.

The registers and other archives of the late medieval English bishops are themselves, therefore, testimony to conscientious, sometimes even dedicated pastoral care. The long ordination lists and records of institutions of priests to churches were the best guarantee that episcopal control of personnel would be maintained, that unsuitable candidates would not be admitted to the ministry and that simony* would be minimised. It seems that canonical standards for the conduct of the priestly office were nearer to realisation in the late fifteenth century than at any time before. Clergy who transgressed the law of the church were admonished, punished and ultimately deprived of their livings. A far more serious view was taken of neglect of the cure of souls than of sexual irregularity, which indeed only came to light if it caused scandal within the community. The bishops and their senior officials responded consistently to the religious needs of the laity, commissioning skilled preachers to tour their dioceses to supplement parochial instruction, licensing private oratories in the houses of the well-to-do or chapels for the inhabitants of outlying hamlets, and administering vows to widows who wished to live in chastity or to men who wished to become hermits. The bishop himself often acted as arbiter and peacemaker in social conflicts and directed the prayers and alms of his subjects to worthy causes by the grant of indulgences. Despite accusations of venality by contemporary critics, diocesan administrators devoted much of their time to pastoral work which brought no profit. There is little to indicate that the vast majority of the English people were dissatisfied with their efforts (**128**).

The episcopate of the century before the Reformation contained no intellectual giants. The most prolific author, indeed, Bishop Reginald Pecock of Chichester (1450–59), was condemned for heresy and deprived of his see, because his relentless application of reason to religion, intended as a counterblast to the Lollards, was carried to extremes, and his ideas were the more dangerous because often presented in English (**50**). The bishops as a group, however, were even better educated than their predecessors: 91 per cent of them were graduates of Oxford or Cambridge, and a high proportion had attained doctorates. Those with degrees in law had the best hope of promotion to the episcopal bench, and theologians normally had to be content with the poorer sees. It has frequently been suggested that this gave the leadership of the church an unfortunately legalistic stamp and that lawyer-bishops were more likely to be constantly absent from their dioceses on royal business. In fact, many of the theologians who were appointed during the reign of Henry VI, when the leaders of dominant aristocratic factions obtained the elevation of their own chaplains, proved less able and conscientious than the generality of lawyers (**37**). It may, indeed, be argued that a university training in law emphasised equity and compassion in its interpretation, and that the canonist, studying a code which embraced every sphere of human activity, had more appreciation of the problems of an ordinary Christian than the theologian who dealt with intellectual concepts. Certainly many eminent late medieval lawyers emerged as excellent diocesans, either during or after their service to the state, as did Beckington at Wells (1443–65) and Pavy at St David's (1485–96).

Fewer bishops in the last century of the medieval church than hitherto had previously been permanent, career civil servants;

rather they executed occasional commissions for the government when their skills were required. An increasing number had experience of diocesan administration before they were raised to the episcopate (**37**). Thomas Goldwell of Norwich (1473–99) had been Commissary-General of Canterbury diocese, Edward Vaughan of St David's (1509–22) had been Official of the diocese of London. In such roles they would necessarily have experienced a wide range of religious and ecclesiastical problems and have dealt with a multitude of sinners, so that on appointment as bishops they were hardly devoid of experience of the church at grass-roots level.

The majority of the bishops were men whose academic training had been devised to furnish them with practical skills, and they did much, from the late fourteenth century onwards, to provide similar opportunities for others. Between 1350 and 1525 nine colleges at Oxford and Cambridge were founded by English bishops, and they acted as advisers in the establishment of others. Many grammar schools also owed their origins to episcopal initiative. Thomas Rotherham, Archbishop of York (1480–1500), for example, established one such at his birthplace in 1483, and Bishop Oldham of Exeter (1505–19) was founder of Manchester Grammar School (**40, 57, 169**). The episcopate, indeed, took a leading part in the educational revolution which occurred in the fifteenth century (**73**). The main purpose of these establishments founded by the bishops was to provide an education for prospective priests; in this way, as much as by their work in court and on visitation, the bishops set standards for clerical performance.

Numerous examples could be presented of scrupulous episcopal conduct. Among Lancastrian appointments, John Carpenter, scholar, royal clerk and Bishop of Worcester (1444–76), devoted himself to the contemporary needs of his diocese, amalgamating three decayed monasteries with larger institutions and establishing at Westbury-on-Trym a collegiate church with a resident schoolmaster, an almshouse and a chantry* served by six aged priests: its constitution was a reflection of his concern for those in need. At Worcester and Bristol he founded public libraries whose custodians were to give open lectures on Scripture, and he licensed numerous graduates to preach throughout the diocese. His surviving injunctions of 1451 reveal a determination to foster proper liturgical practice and good discipline among clerks and layfolk (**132**). Similarly, at Ely, Bishop William Gray (1454–78), an aristocrat, scholar and former servant of king and pope, conscientiously supervised his diocese, conducting ordinations in person and increasing the stipends of vicars who actually served parish churches at the expense of monasteries who received the rectorial* income (**134**).

The pattern is repeated in the early sixteenth century. At Chichester Robert Sherborne (1508–36) overhauled the complex judicial machinery of his diocese in order to centralise authority in his own hands and then used these reformed courts, together with regular visitations, to launch a drive against delinquents, acting firmly against incontinent clergy and incumbents absent without licence, and enforcing the repair of dilapidated churches. Until circumscribed by the onset of the Reformation crisis, he effected a notable improvement in the standard of conduct and religious observance in Sussex (**71**). Bishop Nicholas West of Ely (1515–33), despite continuing diplomatic activity for the king, frequently resided in his diocese, where he strove earnestly to improve standards of clerical learning and discipline by careful examination of candidates for ordination, by visitation and by the convening of regular synods of his clergy, to whom injunctions were issued. His supervision of his diocese has been favourably compared with that of his Protestant successor (**143, 163**).

The records of the diocese of Winchester under Bishop Richard Fox (1501–28), who resigned the keepership of the privy seal in 1516 after a lifetime of service to the Tudors, are voluminous, and reveal assiduous activity by the bishop and his officials in the supervision of monastic houses, the regulation of parochial life and the extirpation of heresy (**18, 49**). Fox's concern that his three previous dioceses had been neglected was, moreover, probably misplaced, for despite his absence his Officials-Principal*, notably Richard Nix, who was himself to become an active bishop of Norwich, had discharged effectively the jurisdictional and administrative duties of the diocesan. The bishops, absent or present, were supported by a staff of highly competent ecclesiastical lawyers who showed efficiency in routine matters and humanity in their judgements. Even during vacancies of sees the spiritual health of the diocese was not neglected, as is shown especially by the meticulous visitation of the diocese of Norwich by Archbishop Morton's commissaries in 1499 (**137**). Where the diocesan was, almost always necessarily, absent, functions restricted to the episcopal order were fulfilled by suffragans*; from the fifteenth century these tended to serve for a long period in one, or at most two neighbouring dioceses, which made for stability and continuity in pastoral work (**175**).

The most detailed work on diocesan administration in early Tudor England is that accomplished by Mrs Bowker on the huge diocese of Lincoln (**6, 33, 34**). She has demonstrated that Bishop Atwater (1514–21) in particular was committed to the work of reform, conducting in person the visitation of 103 rural deaneries and a number of religious house, and presiding in his Court of Audience for half its recorded sessions. From April to September in every year he was constantly on the move, ordaining, visiting and correcting. Only open to question is her assertion that he was 'an unusually conscientious and devoted bishop' (**34**, p. 2), for whenever in recent years a late medieval bishop has been subjected to detailed scrutiny, his reputation has emerged much enhanced.

Leadership of the episcopate was normally and naturally provided by the archbishop of Canterbury, whose provincial court provided a training-ground for the bishops of the next generation. The primatial chair of St Augustine was occupied in the fifteenth century by two outstanding men. Henry Chichele (1414–43), working at first in close association with King Henry V, inspired a 'recovery of nerve among senior churchmen'(**110**, p. 104) who had suffered emotionally and intellectually from the shock of the Great Schism and the initial dangerous assaults of the Lollards. He was a leader in ecclesiastical reform and liturgical innovation designed to combat heretical criticism and to direct lay piety into orthodox channels; he initiated the solution of the pressing problem of graduate unemployment in the church; and he managed, often with the greatest difficulty, to mediate between the demands of a strongly nationalist government and those of the restored Papacy (**52**).

Chichele's successors, although able men, were hampered by the political vicissitudes of England in the mid-fifteenth century, and they led an episcopate whose unity was shattered by aristocratic factionalism. Stability at the head of the church was gradually restored by the appointees of King Edward IV, the most able of whom, John Morton, after masterminding the Tudor coup, became Archbishop of Canterbury (1486–1500). The pressing concerns of governmental business did not distract him from concentrating on ecclesiastical reform, which he pursued vigorously, even aggressively, asserting the rights of Canterbury against the claims of lesser churches and authorities. He was set on the elimination of abuses within the church rather than the defence of peripheral privileges which served to protect only the least reputable members of the clerical order, or those monastic communities which he considered had fallen away from their pristine ideals, but which were still protected by exemption from episcopal authority obtained long before. His policy for reform by centralisation within the traditional structure of the English church, to be effected by an Archbishop of Canterbury acting in concert with the crown, deflected temporarily the hostility of the legal element of Henry VII's council, and probably presented the best hope for the healthy development of the English church (**138**).

Morton's policy was, in its essentials, revived by Thomas Wolsey, whose activities have been seen by some historians as one of the contingent causes of the English Reformation (**39**). Wolsey's career was not entirely unprecedented: the same roles of papal legate* (although not cardinal) and chief minister of the king had been fulfilled in the 1190s by Hubert Walter, Archbishop of Canterbury in the reign of Richard I. He was strongly criticised by contemporary ecclesiastical chroniclers, but he is now appreciated to have been not the creature of the king who wasted the legacy of Thomas Becket, but an effective reformer through administration who achieved much for the church by co-operation with the crown (**36**). The same opportunities for comprehensive action were presented to Wolsey three hundred years later.

There were, of course, anomalies in Wolsey's position. His status in government was, however, a tribute to his abilities – he did supremely well what had been expected by the crown of leading ecclesiastics for at least five hundred years, serving the king in many capacities and doing it, until the final catastrophe, very efficiently. It was inevitable, however, in a faction-ridden court, that he should attract bitter hostility for purely political reasons. The ostentatious pomp of his life-style, while well-suited to a Renaissance court, was the antithesis of the apostolic simplicity which was a model for reform (**39, 80**). The tenure *in commendam** of other sees with the archbishopric of York had only one precedent in post-Conquest England but was common on the Continent, and the administration by him of dioceses held by non-resident aliens was merely a consequence of the policy inaugurated by Henry VII of granting English bishoprics to foreigners useful to the crown. The most glaring abuse may appear to have been the holding by a secular of the great Benedictine abbey of St Albans, yet it was this house which, within Wolsey's memory, had held out against the efforts of Morton to effect general monastic reform, and it may have been the potential threat to his own plans as well as the rich revenues of the house which prompted him to take it into his own hands. Most unfortunate for the cardinal was the longevity of Archbishop Warham of Canterbury, for it was traditional that the southern archbishopric, which Wolsey coveted, should take the leading role within the English church and the smaller province of York generally followed suit. The dispute between Wolsey as legate and the English bishops over probate jurisdiction, which caused such bitterness, was a continuation, in another guise, of that which had raged intermittently between Canterbury and its suffragans* since the thirteenth century over the precise implementation of that custom, unique to England, whereby the church supervised the disposal of the movable goods of the deceased (**71**). That Wolsey claimed to act by legatine rather than by metropolitan* authority was merely an additional argument to be used against him by his opponents.

Whatever his personal faults, and to whatever extent Wolsey was an insular manifestation of the failings seen by contemporary critics in the Renaissance Papacy, his programme, whilst standing within the mainstream of reforming legislation, did contain some novel proposals. His plan for the abolition of minor orders would have resolved a matter of contention, through ecclesiastical legislation, by removing the protection of benefit of clergy from those who contributed little to the church's ministry and from whose ranks came the vast majority of alleged malefactors. The proposed creation of an unspecified number of new bishoprics from the revenues of suppressed monasteries was a recognition of the problems faced by the bishops of vast dioceses such as York, Lincoln and Norwich and was designed to improve pastoral efficiency. In general, however, Wolsey's intention was to effect reforms which had been advocated by generations of English prelates, as is shown by his own constitutions for the province of York, a northern counterpart to Lyndwood's *Provinciale*, the classic statement of canon law for Canterbury.

The justification for the cardinal's statutes proposed in 1519 to the Augustinian canons, which were largely based on the constitutions of Pope Benedict XII of 1334, is provided by their own pessimistic conclusion the previous year that the ruin of all monasticism was imminent. The chief novelty of Wolsey's legislation was that the hitherto exempt* houses of the affiliations of Arrouaise and St Victor, which had avoided any native supervision, were now ordered to attend the Augustinian general chapter*. A year later the legate presented to the provincial assembly of the Benedictine monks a book of statutes designed to reform the order.

33

The response was tepid, as it had been a century earlier when Henry V had urged reform [**doc. 5**]. In his relations with individual houses, Wolsey attempted to enforce the resignation of old and infirm superiors and to undermine free election in order to impose his own nominees – but these were men such as Richard Whiting at Glastonbury, whose rule was so strict that even the royal visitors in 1535 could find no fault with his house. At the nunnery of Wilton the cardinal stood out against the royal will and Boleyn influence to install a worthy abbess. The surviving injunctions of his commissaries for the visitation of religious houses are similar in tenor and tone to those pronounced by numerous English bishops. The suppression of some two dozen convents to provide for his twin educational foundations at Ipswich and Oxford was merely an extension, on a grand scale, of the means adopted by eminent episcopal founders of schools and university colleges since the late fourteenth century. The majority of the communities thus dissolved were so small that the liturgical round, which was the reason for their existence, could not be maintained, and the diversion of their resources to institutions which were socially and educationally useful had thoroughly respectable precedents. The cardinal's plans extended further than this, however, and the bull which he obtained in 1528 authorising the union of monastic houses with less than twelve inmates with their more prosperous and vigorous neighbours was in line with contemporary continental proposals for monastic reform (**56**).

The tragedy, both for humanists and for conservatives who desired reform within the structure of a united and orthodox church, was that Wolsey's apparently genuine and constructive proposals were tainted by his own ambitions and by the suspicion, often corroborated, that they would incidentally bring profit to him. The most enduring reforms which had been implemented in the English church had been those of the papal legates Otto and Ottobuono in the thirteenth century, which were still constantly cited at the end of the Middle Ages. Wolsey sought to act by the same authority, which transcended the boundaries of the provinces of Canterbury and York and extended to the totality of that natural and national unit, the *ecclesia Anglicana*. In addition, he wielded political power far greater than that exercised by the normality of Chancellors. It would not have been easy, as Morton's experience had proved, to have breached the entrenched positions of those exempt* religious houses which rejoiced in privileges centuries-old and now anachronistic, and of those diocesan bishops whose genuine desire for reform was tempered by a fierce determination to preserve their own jurisdictional rights (**140**). That it was possible was proved by the achievement in contemporary Spain of Cardinal Ximenes, who highhandedly carried through reforms which reinvigorated the church of the Catholic Kings (**70**). In England the potential agent of reform was not worthy of the task he set himself, and his enemies were swift to take advantage of his personal failings. Rather than unity, he accidentally promoted dissension, at a crucial time within the leadership of the church. The tradition of episcopal reform was not, however, dissipated, and it is a tribute to the outstanding quality of generations of English bishops that the continuing importance of the episcopate after the breach with Rome is one of the features that sets England apart from continental Protestantism (**144**).

4 The Religious Orders

The underlying problem for the religious orders at the close of the Middle Ages is encapsulated in the answer given in 1519–20 by the Benedictine general chapter to Cardinal Wolsey's demand for more austere observance. A sudden return to rigorous interpretation of the Rule would provoke widespread rebellion and apostasy, recruitment would cease and numerous monasteries would become depopulated [**doc. 5**]. There were in England in 1500 almost nine hundred religious communities, excluding hospitals, which contained some twelve thousand inmates under vows. The total population of England has been estimated at a maximum of 2.6 million, and since five-sixths of the religious were men, at least one in a hundred of the adult male population lived under a religious rule (**57**).

Monasticism had originally been devised as a pathway to perfection for a spiritual elite divorced from the world. In the early Middle Ages, however, the monastic ethos had come to dominate the theology of the western church; the cloister was regarded as the surest, perhaps the only, road to heaven. Communities had gained extensive estates by the gift of lords eager to acquire the celestial benefits won by the prayers of the monks. The vast majority of English monasteries had been founded in the century and a half after the Norman Conquest. Many were poorly endowed and even in their heyday had only a small complement of religious. With the recurrent ravages of plague from the mid-fourteenth century onwards, it became impossible to maintain a full communal life in such houses. Conflicts of personality could ruin internal harmony, while the dramatic increase in agricultural wages made it impossible to maintain financial equilibrium. Many of these minuscule houses had been swept away in the late fourteenth century, when the alien priories, suspect because of their French affiliation, had been suppressed by royal command to endow various notable educational foundations, and this precedent had been followed by bishops who had diverted the resources of small native houses to other more relevant religious purposes.

Wolsey was no innovator in his financing by this means of his two colleges, and much might have been achieved had he been able to implement the papal bull which he obtained on the eve of his fall, authorising him to amalgamate houses with less than twelve inmates with flourishing neighbouring communities. There would have been no diminution of religious vocations or resources, while discipline and observance would have been more easily maintained (**56, 78**).

The larger communities did not face the same problems. A post-Reformation account lovingly describes the full liturgical round of Durham Cathedral Priory whose monks, guardians of St Cuthbert's relics, remained central to the religious life of the north-east (**11**), while Henry VII was content to be buried in the stately grandeur of Westminster Abbey and to entrust his soul to an unceasing round of monastic prayer. Estate management had usually been intelligently adapted to post-plague conditions, and the records of the greater houses bear testimony to their continuing public influence and extensive patronage (**12**). Many monasteries undertook ambitious building programmes in the early Tudor period. These works are manifestations of confidence and stability, but they are also symptomatic of underlying problems. In the later Middle Ages monastic superiors had increasingly withdrawn from their communities to live in their own mansions, such as those built at Hailes and Much Wenlock, and for much of the year they perambulated their estates. Their external life was little different from that of prosperous secular landlords. The greater monasteries were complex business corporations. Many of the community, and inevitably the most able, were heavily committed to the routine administration of the monastery and estate. For these, individual apartments and release from liturgical duties were desirable practical expedients, but such concessions inevitably militated against communal life. The busy men of affairs who abounded in major houses could scarcely be, as St Benedict had intended, dead to the world (**56, 78**).

One index of the general state of the enclosed religious orders is provided by the records of the visitations conducted in the diocese of Coventry and Lichfield between 1515 and 1525 (**16**). The bishop and his deputies visited twenty-nine houses, some moderately prosperous and others tiny and impoverished. In general recruitment was steady, although there was no hope of restoring pre-plague complements. On occasions there are indications of attempts to restrict numbers in order to preserve living standards. In some houses there was difficulty in maintaining the liturgy because so many of the religious had administrative duties, yet if the superior consolidated the various offices in his own hands, as increasingly happened, there was danger of unchecked incompetence or parsimonious tyranny. After a period of bad harvests and savage royal taxation, thirteen houses in 1524 were burdened by debt, yet in most the position improved over the years after the visitor's attentions. Financial pressures had led in two instances to the abandonment of alms for the poor. There were also complaints that individual stipends for clothes and spices had been withdrawn – for if these were contrary to the Rule, they were sanctioned by long usage and papal legislation. Savings might have been made on the wages of servants; the worst example was at Darley, where there were fifteen canons and fifty-seven lay servants. This situation was common to the whole country; it has been estimated that at the Dissolution English monasteries contained 7000 religious and 25,000 laypeople, mostly servants, but also numerous boarders of both sexes, who often enough had secured a financial bargain, akin to a modern annuity, and who inevitably brought their secular interests and pursuits into the world of the cloister.

The duties of superiors frequently took them away from their houses, and the brethren and sisters were hardly isolated from the outside world. Communities all too often split into factions when a new superior was to be elected, and these divisions often persisted – a situation which might lead to apostasy and the attempt of the defeated faction to impose its will from without the walls, even by armed force (**139**). Most offences against discipline were not so dramatic. The most frequent were neglect of the rules of enclosure and of silence, absence from services, the keeping of dogs in the cloister, surly disobedience and incompetence in administration, and perhaps most seriously, a lack of charity towards brethren manifested in gossip and backbiting. There were accusations of sexual misconduct, but only twenty out of three hundred religious examined in this decade were even implicated. Several charges seem to have been made from malice, and at eighteen out of the twenty-nine houses there was not even a whisper of scandal.

The interpretation of such visitation records is a delicate exercise. It must be remembered that the standards demanded were extremely high, and that the basic regulations of the monastic life had been formulated in an age when the cloister provided shelter from the dramatically disintegrating world of the declining Roman empire, whereas now full observance entailed rejection of a society characterised by rising living-standards and increasing domestic amenities. Monastic reformers over the centuries had argued that the primitive observance of the various orders was a norm from which there should be no deviation, but in reality, in an age when recruitment was so wide, and perhaps so indiscriminate in terms of commitment to spiritual excellence, it was hardly surprising that the life of the cloister should be influenced by its wider environment. Visitors, moreover, were rightly intent on detecting breaches of the Rule and rooting out abuses. Sound observance was supposedly the norm and attracted little notice. The great majority of religious were accused of no serious fault. It would be an extremely partial interpretation which accepted at face value all accusations, many of which may have been prompted by rivalry or jealousy, and yet suspected a conspiracy of silence in houses whose occupants universally replied that all was well. A mere catalogue of failings diverts attention from houses such as Burton, where financial management was extremely efficient; Coventry, with its concern for the provision of university education for young monks; or Lilleshall, where the main charge against the new abbot was his rigour (**16**). Nor can visitation returns, even if interpreted unfavourably, be used to demonstrate any sudden decline in the later Middle Ages. No such records survive from the twelfth century, that supposed golden age of monasticism, but references in letters and chronicles give hints of scandals as spectacular, if as isolated, as any in the pre-Reformation period, and the first surviving visitation records, from York diocese at the end of the thirteenth century, reveal a situation little different from that in the early Tudor age (**78**).

This is not to deny that among the religious of the early sixteenth century was manifest the whole range of human weaknesses which are always accentuated within any close-knit residential community. The editor of these West Midlands visitations concludes that the offences reported were symptoms of mediocrity rather than depravity. Consideration of the Suffolk returns of the same epoch has led to the judgement that the 'general picture is one of conscientious if uninspired and pedestrian observance of the Rule, marred by occasional minor scandal and a good deal of run-of-the-mill ill-nature in the cloister' (**64**, p. 133). This view is substantiated by visitations of Butley Priory, which reveal many minor complaints in a community with a good reputation which was, however, as its chronicle emphasises, thoroughly integrated with lay society (**8, 19**). In the huge diocese of Lincoln, containing 111 houses, there were a handful which were thoroughly disorderly, both head and members failing in the whole range of their obligations, but most communities, if scarcely the ascetic 'fortresses of prayer' as which they had been founded centuries before, responded as best they could to episcopal injunctions (**13**). The problem was that there were not enough dedicated religious to sustain proper monastic life in so many houses. The most demanding of modern historians of the religious life has concluded, after consideration of the late fifteenth-century visitations of the exempt* Premonstratensian Order, that there was no extraordinary fervour, but few cases of decadence; on the whole the Premonstratensians were a well-disciplined body whose members, with certain exceptions, lived a tolerably observant life (**56**). None of these visitations, conducted by conscientious ecclesiastics, produced any revelations which would justify the scurrilous attacks of Henry VIII's agents, who were of course commissioned to find pretexts for dissolution.

There is every indication that the generality of religious houses and individuals, if they fell far short of the high ideals of their Rule and of the practice of the spiritual giants of the twelfth century, were little different from the mass of their counterparts of earlier generations. In some houses, indeed, there were signs of renewal. Among the Benedictines, Abbot Kidderminster of Winchcombe (1488–1527) fashioned a community steeped in the best traditions of monastic scholarship, while at Glastonbury numbers were increasing on the eve of the Dissolution; at both these houses there was an intense preoccupation with the tradition of reform of previous centuries (**56, 125**). A group of able Cistercian abbots, led by Marmaduke Huby of Fountains (1494–1526), worked tirelessly for the regeneration which they regarded as essential, and certainly attainable. Their enthusiasm and optimism were scarcely less than that of their twelfth-century predecessors, who similarly had sought during a 'crisis of monasticism' to create a more refined form of spiritual life. Their efforts bore fruit in at least one Cistercian house, Cleeve, where in the 1530s constant steady recruitment produced a community uncomfortably large in relation to its resources, yet even the Dissolution commissioner had to admire the hospitality which was dispensed, greatly to the advantage of the poor (**31, 97**).

Increasingly in the later Middle Ages, however, the enclosed religious orders failed to satisfy the spiritual needs and aspirations of the laity. Their position had initially been undermined by the mendicant* orders of friars. Most monasteries, particularly the large Benedictine and Cistercian houses, were rooted in the countryside as great estate-owners, and if individual monks took a vow of poverty, they were recruited from the upper levels of society and were members of rich corporations. The friars had responded to the urban religious crisis of the thirteenth century, evangelising and ministering in the towns to the alienated poor (**85**). Their new style of preaching and their corporate poverty had won support from all levels of society, and by the fourteenth century monks were on the defensive, constantly seeking to justify their possessions and their withdrawal from the world. By the late fifteenth century the great days of the friars in England were over; they had ceased to dominate the intellectual life of the universities, as they had for the previous two hundred years, and they attracted vituperation from poets and satirists for their gluttony, lechery and avarice – although such writers were normally secular* priests who feared loss of revenue and influence to the mendicants (**84**). Their decline has certainly been exaggerated, however, for until the Dissolution a far greater proportion of wills included bequests to the friars, often to all four orders, than to the enclosed religious. Traditionally support for monks, canons and nuns had come from the aristocracy and gentry; twelfth-century and thirteenth-century charters reveal that few such families failed in benefactions to at least one monastery. The wills which survive in abundance from the last medieval century reveal that this support had significantly diminished, being maintained largely by lords who were the ancestral patrons of monasteries and by those who had kinsfolk therein, to whom bequests were often, in contravention of the Rule, specifically directed. The upper ranks of English society had ceased to look to the monks and canons for those prayers, increasingly urgently required, which would ease the passage to heaven of the benefactor's soul (**91, 127, 172**). Such intercession had been the *raison d'être* of monasteries; now it was eschewed, and those who could afford lavish bequests for prayer normally looked elsewhere, to the friars or the secular* clergy. There was little overt hostility to monasticism. Men of substance would dine or hunt with the local abbot or prior and would sit alongside him on commissions of the peace – but to the spiritual ministrations of his house they were likely to be indifferent.

It would be facile to state that the monastic order had gone into decline. It had, rather, remained static while the world had changed about it. Since the early thirteenth century the church had encouraged laymen to search for a more personal, interiorised relationship with God. Located firmly within this tradition, the writings of late fourteenth-century English mystics such as Richard Rolle and Walter Hilton, which achieved wide popularity, were not a reaction against formal religion, but an attempt to communicate to a wider lay audience the authors' deep experience of the love of God and to encourage them to the imitation of Christ (**17, 51**). These writings were completely orthodox, yet their emphasis on the intense relationship between Christ and the individual sinner left little place for the vicarious role of the traditional monk, who took upon his shoulders the sins of the world and rendered the debt of mankind to a God conventionally portrayed as a stern judge.

It is significant that the only monastic houses which continued to attract substantial benefactions were those which fostered this new form of personal piety and encouraged individual, yet entirely orthodox, religious initiative among the literate laity. There had been a small spate of Carthusian foundations in late fourteenth-century England, when large-scale endowment of other orders had already ceased. The physical plan of Carthusian houses, which can still be seen at Mount Grace in Yorkshire, reveals their ethos. The monks lived the life of hermits, devoting themselves to meditation in private cells in which they ate and slept, coming together only for Mass and chapter* meeting. Their life-style was designed to encourage deep personal spirituality within a communal structure which provided safeguards against religious excess, and in this sense the charterhouses provided a model for the church at large. The Carthusians disseminated English spiritual writings first of all to their patrons in the circle of the royal court, and by the later fifteenth century to a wider audience of educated laypeople who sought to live a life of spiritual commitment while remaining in the world (**56, 110**).

The greatest of the Carthusian foundations was that at Sheen, established by Henry V and twinned with a community of Bridg-ettine nuns at nearby Syon. This profoundly religious king had intended his houses to serve as a bulwark against heresy and an exemplar of the integration of intense private devotion with public religious ceremony. They served as the channel for the popular-isation in England of those new modes of piety from the Low Countries known as the *Devotio Moderna* (see page 6). The nuns of Syon have a particular significance, for the English nunneries in general were the least satisfactory element of the monastic order, the repository of young ladies surplus to the marriage-market whose conduct and demeanour often left much to be desired. The Bridgettines provided a model of female piety for those who chose to remain in the world, demonstrating that despite their exclusion from the ministry of the altar, women could play a positive role in religion while avoiding the frenzied excesses of mystics like Margery Kempe, whose enthusiasm had incited the aggressively orthodox citizens of Canterbury to contemplate burning her (**5, 110**). The continuing influence of Syon is revealed by the popularity of the devotional works of Richard Whitford, one of the priests attached to the convent in the early sixteenth century. His most influential book, *The Work for Householders*, published on the eve of the Dissolution, provided sound practical advice for the fostering of piety based on a monastic model within a lay household (**56**).

Criticism of the monastic order was nothing new in early Tudor England. It was no greater in volume and acerbity than in the twelfth century, when the early Cistercians had lambasted the Benedictines for their wealth and luxury, and had in turn been criticised by the clerical courtiers of Henry II for their avarice. The essential difference now, perhaps, was that an increasing number of literate laypeople were themselves practising an enhanced form of religious observance; the only specifically monastic virtue appeared to be celibacy. Those legislators who had allowed the monasteries to take a more relaxed line on such things as personal money, increased privacy and the eating of meat, had doubtless been realistic, but in the early sixteenth century the educated and pious laity could measure contemporary practice against the demands of the original Rule of St Benedict, translated into English by Bishop Fox. Frequent economic and social intercourse with the religious must have convinced intelligent and influential laymen that monks and canons were scarcely different from themselves in lifestyle and aspirations (**140**). There was little open antagonism, but also little conviction that the majority of monasteries served a useful spiritual function. That the ideal was still respected is demonstrated by the devotion of the most perceptive and educated of the laity to Syon and the charterhouses, which housed a spiritual elite who from their austere seclusion provided sympathetic inspiration for lay devotion.

5 The Parish Clergy

The spiritual and social efficacy of the English church was largely dependent on the performance of those clergy who served in the parishes, either as beneficed rectors* and vicars*, with security of tenure, or as assistant chaplains. For the vast majority of the English people, living in isolated rural communities, these men were the only effective representatives of the universal church. A travelling friar or a preacher of indulgences might occasionally pass through the parish, a monk from the house which was their landlord might hold a manorial court, or they might see the archdeacon's* official conducting a visitation or a suffragan bishop conducting a confirmation; but the parish priest was ever-present – the dispenser of sacraments, religious instruction and moral guidance. The parochial clergy were subjected to harsh criticisms from generations of preachers and from the humanists of the early sixteenth century, which are encapsulated in Dean Colet's Convocation sermon of 1512 (**27, 63, 75, 140**). There certainly were some clergy who fell below the high standards set by the medieval theologians and canon lawyers, but there are strong indications that the vast majority fulfilled their ministry conscientiously and to the satisfaction of their flock.

The English church was an exceedingly rich institution; the quarter of the landed wealth of the country which it had held at the time of Domesday Book had expanded in the next four hundred years. These resources, however, were concentrated in the hands of the monastic, cathedral and collegiate bodies. There were a few very lucrative parochial livings; the best of all was probably Winwick in Lancashire, valued at £102 per annum (**44**). These were the preserve of noble families and highly-favoured royal clerks, and they were the exception. It has been calculated that around 1500 an income of £15 a year was a necessary minimum for any incumbent who employed an assistant chaplain, and that even if he served the cure himself without any help, £10 a year was required to maintain a barely decent standard of living and to discharge a multitude of obligations. In practice less than a quarter of all English livings were worth £15, and very many were worth less than £7. In the diocese of Coventry and Lichfield, which was typical of the country as a whole, 79 per cent of benefices were valued at less than £15, 60 per cent at less than £10 and 10 per cent at less than £5. In Leicestershire too 60 per cent of all benefices were worth £10 or less. Over one third of all the parish churches in England, moreover, were appropriated* to monasteries or other ecclesiastical corporations who took the bulk of the income, the rectorial portion, a smaller part being reserved for the vicar who actually served the parish. Almost 90 per cent of English vicarages were valued at less than £15, and 70 per cent of them brought in only between £5 and £10 a year. Appropriation, however, cannot be blamed entirely for the poverty of parochial livings, for in the diocese of Coventry and Lichfield half the livings worth less than £10 were rectories unattached to any monastery. In short, the great majority of those English clergy who were fortunate enough to obtain a benefice* were not wallowing in luxury, but rather were struggling to make ends meet (**46, 79**).

The demands on the incumbent's income were many – the upkeep of the chancel of the church and of his rectory or vicarage, the wages of servants and a chaplain if one was employed, frequently the support of aged parents, and the payment of customary dues to the bishop and archdeacon*. A third of his income should in theory have been dispensed in alms and hospitality, although few can have fulfilled this ideal. The rate and frequency of royal taxation, moreover, was constantly increasing. An income of £10 a year could easily shrink to £4 net after the discharge of these burdens. The circumstances of the majority of incumbents around 1500 were straitened, even before the ravages of inflation in the early sixteenth century. Those country rectors with extensive glebe* which they exploited themselves or let out on short leases were able to maintain their real income. Those who had granted long leases on their lands or who occupied urban churches with little land attached, and those vicars who received a fixed stipend from monastic rectors, were in appalling difficulties. The collection in full of tithe* income became a more urgent necessity than hitherto, yet tithe-payers themselves, unless they were the possessors of substantial estates, were equally hard-pressed, for in the second decade of the sixteenth century real wages were falling for the first time in several centuries. What is perhaps surprising is that there were not far more bitter disputes over the collection of tithes, and that the clash of economic interests did not result in a general withdrawal of allegiance from the church (**46, 72, 79, 131**).

The economic situation of those clergy who remained without a benefice* – who were the majority – was even worse. For stipendiary chaplains the late fourteenth century had been a golden age. In the aftermath of the Black Death, when their numbers had decreased and the demand for masses for the dead had soared, the survivors had been able to demand enhanced stipends, and legislation to limit their wages had the air of desperation. In the early sixteenth century their successors were competing to earn enough to eke out a living. Chaplains very rarely earned more than £6 13s 4d (£6 67p), which was the statutory maximum fixed in the early fifteenth century; and in the meantime the cost of living had risen considerably. The average income of assistant clergy in the diocese of Lincoln was £5 3s 2d (£5 16p) a year, but in many areas it was less than this. In Lancashire, for example, the average was only £2 9s 2d (£2 46p), and about one fifth of chaplains in this county received less than £1 a year from their regular employment. The minimum for survival was probably about £3 a year, but by the end of the fifteenth century an income of £2 was subject to tax of 3s 4d (17p). In areas like Lancashire, with a far-flung population and large rural parishes, the services of such chaplains were essential for the maintenance of pastoral care; the four thousand communicants of Liverpool, for example, were dependent on the ministrations of four chantry* priests. Despite their social utility, many chaplains were reduced to a frantic search for supplementary sources of income, either in secular employment or by the celebration of private masses. The funeral of a great man who had provided extravagantly for prayers for his soul might act as a magnet for poor priests from many miles around. When Dean Colet in his Convocation sermon accused such men of inordinate greed, he was echoing a long tradition of criticism which may have been valid when first extensively ventilated a century and a half before, but bore no relation to the contemporary condition of a 'clerical proletariat' which was economically depressed but which in general served well the religious needs of the laity (**44, 47, 72**).

There had been a manpower crisis in the English church in the early fifteenth century, perhaps because of disillusionment caused by the schism in the Papacy, in which case the fall in clerical recruitment was a passive counterpart to the active criticism of the church by the Lollards. In the north, where heresy made little impact, the decline was not nearly as steep as in the south and midlands (**161, 176**). In the second half of the century, however, there was a marked increase in candidates for ordination, and this was sustained almost to the eve of the Reformation. The population of England in 1520 was approximately the same as in 1420, but in several dioceses which have been examined clerical recruitment was very much higher (**131**). The financial prospects for the great majority of ordinands were hardly enticing. Of 2600 secular priests ordained in Lincoln diocese between 1495 and 1520, some 60 per cent had no benefice* to support them. Probably less than half of those lacking family connections or influential patrons would ever obtain a living, and for those fortunate enough to acquire even a poor benefice it might take between ten and twenty years (**33, 104**). Very many would struggle to survive by the celebration of the multitude of private masses which were financed by all levels except the poorest of the laity. That society was in the early sixteenth century producing enough priests to satisfy spiritual aspirations, as it had not done a century before, is a mark of confidence in the efficacy of conventional religion (**131**). Complaints of the humanists, such as Sir Thomas More, that quality had given way to quantity in recruitment to the priesthood, fail to take account either of the strong demand for intercessory prayer or of the obvious implication that healthy recruitment was an indication of the high regard in which the priesthood was held in the country as a whole.

The multitude of chaplains seeking employment ensured that the non-residence of a proportion of the incumbents of England's rectories would not have serious consequences for the church's ministry. The number of absentee rectors in those dioceses whose records have been analysed varies between 10 and 25 per cent. It is probably reasonable to estimate that one in six parish churches was not served personally by the man to whom the revenues had been granted and the cure of souls entrusted. There were various reasons for absence, the most common of which was pluralism. Although canon law required that a cleric should hold only one benefice which entailed the exercise of pastoral care, many dispensations were issued by the Papacy to 'sublime and literate persons', members of aristocratic or other powerful families, or those distinguished by their learning [**doc. 3a**]. A splendid example of a man who fulfilled both criteria is John Talbot, an illegitimate member of the family of the Earls of Shrewsbury, who between 1498 and 1518 obtained three doctorates at Oxford. Clerks engaged in the royal service were similarly favoured; the young Wolsey, for example, was granted two papal dispensations before his elevation to the episcopate. Bishops, hard-pressed to provide decently for their learned administrative staff, might also petition Rome to obtain the same concession for their vicar-general or chancellor (**33, 47, 79**). The impression gained from the records is that most of those who were provided by their pluralism with a comfortable or good living were fulfilling a useful function in society, and that the number of parochial livings which they might hold was carefully regulated. Pluralists, moreover, were not all affluent. The impoverishment of so many livings, and the difficulty of amalgamating neighbouring churches because of the involvement of patrons, caused many bishops to tolerate and even encourage licensed pluralism as the only way to provide even a moderately decent income for clergy who were perhaps well-qualified and worthy, but who lacked the patronage of a great man. An analysis of Leicestershire pluralists between 1520 and 1540 has revealed that of a total of twenty-nine, a third had very good livings, a third had a tolerable income of £10–15 from two churches, but a third were still struggling economically despite their pluralism (**129**).

Bishops and their officials were careful to regulate non-residence. Licences granted by them for absence for study were limited in duration and had to be renewed frequently, and unlicensed absentees were forced into residence by the threat of sequestration of their revenues. There are indications in visitation records that the authorities would act even in the case of legitimate absenteeism if they found the pastoral care of the parish to be neglected, but this was very seldom the case. Most of the rich Lancashire livings held by non-residents were served by two or three assistant clergy, and in the diocese of Lincoln between 1514 and 1520, out of 1085 churches visited and in spite of 25 per cent absenteeism, there were only seven cases where the parish was not served by a curate or he too was absent. In neither of these large areas, moreover, is there any indication that the assistant clergy behaved worse or served their flock less satisfactorily than the incumbents, or that they were more prone to misdemeanour or neglect in parishes where they were unsupervised than in those where the rector was resident (**33, 44**). As long as there was no shortage of clergy and provided that the episcopal authorities were vigilant, pluralism and non-residence did not adversely affect the ministrations of the church in the parishes.

The most common accusation against the clergy was probably sexual immorality. This is understandable, considering human propensity for gossip and the strict canonical regulations enforcing celibacy. The easiest way for any disgruntled parishioner to cause trouble for his priest was to initiate a rumour. In fact, however, the proportion of parish clergy either accused or convicted of immorality is remarkably low. In Winchester archdeaconry in 1527–28 11 clergy from 230 churches came to the notice of the authorities on this score, and 4 of these cleared themselves of the charge. Within the jurisdiction of York Minster an average of 1.5 per cent of the clergy were arraigned before the court for sexual offences in any year. There were only five allegations of immorality from 487 Suffolk parishes in 1499. In Lincoln diocese between 1514 and 1520, from 1006 parishes visited, 126 incumbents were reported to have a woman, but in only 26 cases (2.5 per cent) was the accusation proved or very likely true – all parsonages contained female servants whose presence provided opportunity for gossip. In the same period only 12 chaplains were arraigned for incontinence. There is no correlation between sexual offences and neglect of priestly duties within the parish (**33, 35, 49, 137**). The church was never completely successful in the imposition of celibacy – it would have been remarkable if it had been – but the clerical dynasties which had in the earlier Middle Ages passed churches from father to son had been eliminated, and incontinence was not a scandal which threatened the status of the priesthood. It is always possible to compile a collection of entertainingly scandalous cases, but this proves very little. The relatively small number of recorded instances of immorality demonstrates either creditably strict adherence to a very demanding code, or a great deal of popular tolerance of faults regarded in canon law as very serious.

The parish clergy were, understandably, even less prone to crime than to sin. The old issue of benefit of clergy, which had in the 1160s provoked the clash between Becket and Henry II, was still alive. That a clerk convicted of a felony before the king's justices might plead his clergy (demonstrable by the ability to read, which with the passing of each generation became a less meaningful test) and thus avoid the death penalty was probably generally resented, and certainly prompted Parliamentary legislation designed to curb this abuse. The offender did not, in fact, escape scot-free, being incarcerated in an episcopal prison, in extreme cases for life, usually for months or years, before being allowed to clear himself by the oath of a dozen or more clerks that they believed in his innocence. The evidence of those episcopal registers which are most informative on this matter suggests that the extent of the problem was exaggerated, and also that few of these clerks were in major orders, and so were not those who would serve in a parish in any capacity. The vast majority were literate laymen, often married, who had entered one of the minor orders but were in effect employed in entirely secular occupations. Of sixty-two offenders proceeding to compurgation* in York diocese between 1452 and 1530 only six were 'professional clergy', and none of those in the bishop of Lincoln's prisons in 1509 could have been involved in pastoral work. Parochial clergy were, of course, arraigned in the royal courts, but a cursory examination of the records suggests that many cases resulted from injury or death inflicted in self-defence in those brawls characteristic of this violent society, while a false indictment for rape under the common law was an even better way of settling a personal score than an accusation of incontinence before an ecclesiastical tribunal (**47, 86**).

Allegations of neglect were more common, but by far the most frequent manifestation of this was the decayed condition of the chancel of the church or of the parsonage. In view of the economic condition of the clergy it is hardly surprising that many were incapable of effecting major structural repairs. In appropriated* churches, moreover, these were often the responsibility of the religious house which held the rectory rather than of the vicar. In Suffolk in 1499 only eleven cases of neglect of the fabric were reported, but in selected deaneries of Lincoln diocese between 1517 and 1520 one third of the churches had some defect in the fabric or furniture of the chancel, although half of these were the responsibility of the appropriators. There was perhaps little incentive for the non-resident rector to repair his parsonage, but the ten Kentish vicars in 1511 who lived in decayed homes can hardly have enjoyed the experience (**28, 33, 137**). The visitors and courts did enforce repairs by sequestration of revenues, but the cost must have reduced many poorer incumbents to penury, consuming their negligible surplus for several years.

Far rarer was any neglect of pastoral duties which can be attributed to the personal shortcomings of the parish priest. In the diocese of Lincoln between 1514 and 1521 there were complaints from parishioners that they were not adequately served in religion from only forty-one out of 1006 churches visited (4 per cent); in five of these this was due to the old age or infirmity of the priest. Complainants alleged that services were irregular in time or manner of performance, that the sacraments were not administered properly or at all, or that the local priest failed to preach or visit the sick. In Canterbury diocese in 1511 the most heartfelt complaint against clergy in 260 parishes was that one rector denied his flock consecrated bread and holy water and was malicious to them, and that due to the negligence of a vicar a woman had died without confession or communion (**28, 33**). It was cases such as these, where the parish priest denied to his flock the sacraments which led to salvation, and thus in the grossest way failed in charity, which caused bitter resentment, but they were few and far between. Certainly the inhabitants of 96 per cent of the parishes of one of the largest dioceses in England (Lincoln) did not wish to complain, when given the opportunity during visitation, about the liturgical or pastoral performance of the priest who cared for their spiritual welfare, be he incumbent or parochial chaplain.

It may be argued, of course, that the expectations of parishioners were too low, that they were concerned only with the mechanics of ritualised religion and had no concern for the quality of the instruction which was offered to them. The general level of clerical education was, however, probably higher than has traditionally been supposed. Some graduates, including those of Oxford and Cambridge colleges founded in the fifteenth century with the specific intention of training young priests in theology, did serve in the parishes. Other parish clergy had attended university without proceeding to a master's degree. Some cathedrals at least, as has been demonstrated for Exeter, acted as educational centres, some of whose products went out into the dioceses. Above all, the explosion of grammar and reading schools in the later Middle Ages provided opportunities for far more young men than hitherto to obtain with relative ease the knowledge necessary for a rural priest. Despite the complaint of Chancellor Melton of York in the early sixteenth century that candidates for ordination were subject to inadequate examination, there is evidence from several dioceses that it was far more than perfunctory. That the suitability of priests for a parochial living was investigated, in one diocese at least, is demonstrated by Bishop West of Ely's order to two new incumbents to improve their education if they were to retain their benefices (**1, 3, 143**). Clerical wills reveal the ownership by parish priests of books, both manuscripts and the products of the new printing presses. The proportion in the diocese of Ely between 1500 and 1519 was 45 per cent, probably high because of the proximity of Cambridge University, but it has been estimated that the possession of books by 25 per cent of all clergy engaged in parochial work, including the unbeneficed, would be 'a very cautious estimate' (**47**, p. 88). In view of the very high price of books in relation to consumables, this figure is surprisingly high. Many owned only service books, but others had copies of one of those manuals for parish priests and confessors or of those preaching aids which had appeared in profusion in the fourteenth century (**76**). The *Golden Legend* of saints' lives was particularly popular, for it provided a collection of splendid moral examples for sermons. There is very little evidence of interest in the new humanist learning – the York rector who had a Greek dictionary and a work by Erasmus was utterly exceptional (**115**). The humanist circle of London and the universities would doubtless have agreed with the modern judgement that early Tudor clerics had a 'predominantly medieval and narrow mentality' (**47**, p. 90); yet there is little to suggest that the great majority of them were not well fitted to provide that instruction in the moral principles of the Christian religion which the legislation of the church required should be taught, and they were not so far removed from their flocks by intellect or by education that they were incapable of comprehending the roots of those social problems which the pastoral manuals urged them to be active in resolving. A learned sermon based on Hebrew and Greek exegesis might have been appreciated in the intellectual milieu of Sir Thomas More, but would have been totally incomprehensible in thousands of English parish churches. A university training in the new learning, as much as in the old scholasticism, might have driven a wedge between priest and people. As a fifteenth-century treatise insisted, what was required for effective parochial work was moral worth and wisdom rather than extensive knowledge (**133**).

The sweeping charges made by Dean Colet in 1512 against the generality of the English clergy were, therefore, in one sense unfounded and in another misconceived (**140**). That we know so much about the failings of a small percentage of parish priests is due to the constant effort of the ecclesiastical authorities to maintain the high standards of the canon law and of the manuals of pastoral theology, whose ideals probably came nearer to realisation in the fifty years before the Reformation than at any other time in the Middle Ages. Serious complaints against miscreant clergy are more than balanced by records of conscientious service extending over many years, culminating in retirement on a very small pension, or more often by death in harness and with bequests to the fabric of the church and to the poor of the parish. If the well-endowed pluralist was little concerned with the good estate of the parishes from which he derived his income, the inhabitants suffered little, for those who actually exercised the ministry proved in general to be labourers worthy of their very modest hire.

6 The Church Courts and the English People

The canon law of the church is a compendium of detailed legislation by which the divine law, revealed to mankind in the Bible, is translated into an enforceable code of Christian behaviour. It is, therefore, a branch of theology designed for practical application, but it is also a reflection of the common assumptions of society which regulate every sphere of human activity. In the medieval world ecclesiastical law was concerned not exclusively with the government of the church or the determination of belief; it expressed a norm for sexual, commercial and political conduct, and it provided sanctions against transgressors. In the late twelfth century, for example, the complicated customs of marriage were clarified and humanised in a series of papal rulings which served to create an ideal of Christian matrimony which protected the rights of the individual, particularly of women, against the property interests of the family. Papal decrees, applied in local ecclesiastical courts, outlined a system for the relief of the poor far more humanitarian than that of post-Reformation England. In almost every sphere canon law served both to mould and to maintain the ideals of the society within which it operated, however often they were contravened by individuals (**69, 82, 85**). It was not an alien code imposed on England from without, as implied by Henry VIII's government when for political reasons it sought to bring an end to the practice and study of Roman canon law; rather it was a legislative interpretation of religious attitudes, in the formulation of which Englishmen – as papal counsellors, papal judges-delegate and academic lawyers – had been extremely influential.

The formative era of the law of the church had been from the late eleventh to the early fourteenth centuries, but its study and practice were far from moribund on the eve of the Reformation. In 1430 Dr William Lyndwood completed his *Provinciale*, a digest of the constitutions of the archbishops of Canterbury, which were local statements of the universal canon law; it enjoyed a dozen early printings. Innumerable printed copies of the standard continental canonical textbooks were imported into England. The canon-law schools of Oxford and Cambridge continued to flourish, their products acting as judges in a hierarchy of tribunals ranging from the provincial courts of the archbishops through the diocesan courts down to those local courts of bishops' commissaries, archdeacons* and the various jurisdictions of monasteries and cathedrals before which the majority of English people, unless they were of elevated status, were likely to appear [**doc. 6**]. At every level the canon lawyers seem to have administered justice fairly and impartially, with more regard to the spirit than to the letter of the law, as did the most distinguished of their number who presided in the royal courts of Chancery and Requests, where the rigour of the common law was tempered by considerations of equity (**174**). In many dioceses there is evidence from the fifteenth and early sixteenth century of reform of the structure and procedure of the courts, designed to expedite business and improve efficiency (**164**). It appears that in the late fifteenth century the ecclesiastical courts were dealing with a greater volume of cases than ever before.

The business of the courts

The business which came before the ecclesiastical courts may be divided into three categories: office cases, brought by the ecclesiastical authorities against suspected malefactors, akin to a criminal prosecution in the royal courts; instance cases, brought at the instance of a party, the equivalent of civil litigation; and probate business, arising from the English custom whereby the church supervised the disposal of the movable goods of deceased persons. The division, however, is not clear-cut. With regard to office prosecutions, it would be a mistake to see the court as an oppressive institution, with an agent in every village in the person of the priest, which sought to impose alien, ecclesiastical standards on lay society. Very many cases stemmed from visitation, but the offender was usually presented to the visitor by the churchwardens, acting as representatives of the community and declaring the common opinion of the neighbours of the accused. At Chesham in 1521 forty angry women dragged into the court another alleged to be a common scandal-monger; at Lichfield in 1466 the evidence against one prostitute was that she made so much noise at night that her neighbours could not sleep (**10, 31**). These are clear and typical instances of the manner in which a local community would use the church courts as a mechanism of social control.

In every lesser court whose records have been analysed sexual offences predominate among the office cases. Some 90 per cent of the business of the York dean and chapter court between 1387 and 1494 concerned adultery, fornication or similar offences, and 110 out of 141 charges brought against laypeople in the Canterbury consistory court in 1474 related to sexual irregularities (**35, 94**). The celibate judges showed remarkable tolerance and humanity in their handling of such cases. They were well aware that accusations could stem from malice and were not swift to convict. In the London commissary court between 1471 and 1493 33 per cent of all prosecutions were for adultery, but only 8 per cent of those charged were convicted. In the early sixteenth century the conviction rate rose, varying from 19 to 33 per cent in any year; this rise seems clearly related to the more rigorous procedure and higher conviction rate in defamation cases (**95**).

Fornication was less serious than adultery, because it did not involve the theft of the rights of a third party. The earlier practice of threatening fornicators with enforced marriage if they sinned again, common in the thirteenth century, was now only applied in the case of repeated intercourse between the same parties; it had been realised that marriage should not be used as a penal sanction, because of the canonical requirement of free consent (**48**). Threat of a heavy penance was, however, used in Suffolk in 1499 to induce one man to marry his illicit partner, because she wished it, and another man was compelled to offer financial compensation to a girl he had seduced (**137**). The judges sought to make provision for the offspring of such unions; from almost every court there are instances of convicted fornicators being required to make provision for the confinement of the woman and the upbringing of the child.

There are isolated cases of prostitution in every court book. At Newmarket in 1499, for example, two sisters operating from a tavern apparently had a monopoly, but they fled before the visitor arrived, probably much to the relief of their clients, who were likely to be denounced as fornicators had they appeared in court (**137**). It is only in London, however, that prostitution and pimping appear as a major problem. The church courts had little success in the control of commercial sex in the capital. In a sample of 337 prosecutions between 1471 and 1514 only ten prostitutes confessed, and many caught in the act were able to clear themselves with the help of their neighbours' oaths that they believed in their innocence. Many simply failed to appear in court, and the sanction of excommunication would probably hold few terrors for those living in the London underworld. The civic authorities, dissatisfied with the record of the church courts, commenced in the 1480s a campaign to clean up the city, and prostitutes were set in the pillory or ducking-stool (**95**). Here it was the leniency and ineffectiveness of the ecclesiastical courts in dealing with sexual misdemeanours which prompted resentment. Elsewhere, in the countryside and in small towns where the canon-law judges were naturally more successful in dealing with such matters, there is no evidence of hostility from the community as a whole and every indication that the correction of sexual offenders and other troublemakers, such as scolds and gossips, was generally welcomed.

The miscellaneous nature of other correctional cases is well illustrated by those brought after the 1499 Suffolk visitation: failure to attend church, chattering during services, the use of superstitious arts, desertion of spouse, failure to pay tithe, illicit occupation of church lands, and sowing discord among neighbours; and single cases of breach of marriage contract, blasphemy, theft of a mortuary offering, and allowing a horse to foul the churchyard (**137**). The most common of these charges was non-attendance at church, but this generally indicates only laziness in those who preferred to lie in bed, or greed in the case of those who plied their trade on Sundays and major festivals, rather than any doubt as to the efficacy of the sacraments. Occasional drives against Sunday trading were launched, for example at Canterbury in 1519, but in London prosecutions of shoemakers and poulterers, apparently the worst offenders, usually ended in a warning rather than penance. The use of superstitious arts, although often described as heretical, was a manifestation rather of primitive folk beliefs which had co-existed with Christianity since the Conversion – credence in the ability to cause harm, to heal or to discover buried treasure by magical means – than of any conscious rejection of orthodox belief; indeed, holy water or Eucharistic wafers were considered to have particularly effective magical powers if they could be removed from the church. Such offenders were punished with more than customary rigour and publicity, but those like the Kent woman cited in 1525 for divining the future from the croaking of frogs, or the Suffolk girl who believed that spirits transported her physically to the tomb of Becket, represented no real threat to the structure of religion or society (**89, 94, 95, 137**) [**doc. 6**].

Among instance cases, a very substantial proportion in the fifteenth century were suits for breach of faith; the majority of these concerned commercial transactions and were, in reality, actions for recovery of debt. Since restitution was an essential part of penance, the creditor hoped to recover his money upon the conviction of his opponent. A high percentage of such cases, in fact, ended in arbitration and compromise; thus, although to modern eyes these cases appear to have little to do with religion, the church courts were fulfilling their traditional role of re-establishing peace between Christians. This category of business evaporated in the early sixteenth century when the secular courts began to recognise oral contracts and creditors turned to them in very large numbers because they had more hope of obtaining full payment of their dues, enforced by threat of imprisonment. It was the institution of a procedure more favourable to aggrieved parties which led to the desertion of the church courts by commercial creditors, rather than any obvious hostility to ecclesiastical jurisdiction, which had been extensively utilised until a more effective alternative was provided (**94, 95, 123, 164**).

The other main category of instance business was charges of defamation. In this tight-knit society good repute was of the greatest importance [**doc. 6**]. Occasionally defamatory words might impute heresy or a crime answerable in the royal courts, which might have appalling consequences, but inevitably most slurs were sexual – variations on the theme of whore or bawd. In London in the later fifteenth century it was very difficult to obtain a conviction; in such matters too the courts encouraged compromise. Even when, under lay pressure, evasion of a defamation charge was made more difficult, the conviction rate rose only to 12 per cent. The courts did, however, provide a forum for the ventilation of grievances. Even those acquitted had to pay a dismissal fee, so were in some small way punished, while simply by bringing an action the offended party had done much to clear his or her name. Again, the courts did much to restore peace within the community (**94, 95, 123**).

Paradoxically, in the light of Henry VIII's complaints about his own treatment, the operation of the church courts is probably seen at its best in the sphere of marriage litigation. Matrimonial cases constituted a much smaller proportion of the courts' business than in the thirteenth century, simply because the church's teaching on marriage had become much more widely accepted. But among those still brought there was a higher percentage of petitions for annulment, which suggests that simple repudiation of a partner without due legal process had become socially unacceptable. Alleged reasons for the dissolution of the marriage were carefully investigated, be it the discovery of kinship previously unknown to the parties or the intolerable drunkenness of the wife. The judges strove to re-establish harmony whenever possible, otherwise to arrive at the best possible settlement for both parties, taking special care to provide for deserted wives and children. Settlements strictly illegal in canon law were allowed if they seemed equitable to the judges. In this most delicate of all areas the courts proceeded quickly and humanely, and the historian of medieval marriage litigation reached the verdict that there is much to admire in the conduct of judges and lawyers (**48**).

The third category of business was probate jurisdiction. The last testament of the deceased came before an ecclesiastical court for ratification before the executors could dispose of his movable goods as he had willed. This was normally uncontentious; it did not involve prosecution or litigation. Accusations of abuse in this sphere of jurisdiction, however, were one of the main strands of the Commons' Supplication against the Ordinaries of 1532 (**27**): there were long delays, executors were cited to far-distant courts, and excessive fees were charged. Examination of court records has suggested that these accusations were unjustified. The Bucking-hamshire archdeaconry* records indicate that probate was often granted only days after death and that the court traversed the county to deal with testamentary business. The episcopal courts of the dioceses of Chichester, Lincoln and Norwich processed this business swiftly: at Chichester, for example, 80 per cent of wills were proved within three months. A sample of Bedfordshire wills shows minimal delay even in the Prerogative Court of Canterbury, which dealt with larger estates spread over more than one diocese. There is abundant evidence that courts were using the sliding scale of fees established by Archbishop Stratford in the mid-fourteenth century; for the smallest estates liable to charges, one-thirtieth of the value was levied, for middling estates one-eightieth, and for those valued at over £100 only 1 per cent (though in addition scribal and summoners' fees were payable). While these fees bore most heavily on the estates of poorer testators, in no case could they be considered excessive, especially when compared with the rate of royal taxation on movables. In short, it may be said that few heirs or executors suffered hardship because of the testamentary jurisdiction of the English church (which continued in only slightly modified form after the Reformation), but that in total the church received from this source significant revenues which financed other essential and non-profitable functions of the courts (**10, 21, 49, 95, 103**).

The effectiveness of the courts

The Commons in 1532 complained that in all categories of business persons were cited to courts far distant from their homes. There is, however, much evidence to the contrary in the records of the archdeacons' officials who regularly moved across their jurisdictions holding courts in small country towns. In Suffolk in 1499 the archbishop's commissary in six weeks held twenty-seven sessions at twenty-three different locations. For the malefactor, the constant proximity of such judges must have been disturbing. In Buckinghamshire it was rare for a defendant to have to travel more than seven miles; a citation to a royal court would normally involve a far longer journey. The Court of Audience of the bishop of Lincoln was held at various episcopal manors across the diocese, and the judge showed himself sympathetic to problems of transport, particularly of those old or ill (**6, 10, 49, 94, 137**). Neither is there any evidence from Lincoln diocese that, as was alleged, summoners charged higher fees the further they had to travel to deliver a citation. At Lincoln, indeed, all fees were substantially lower than was claimed in the Commons' Supplication, and in London court charges remained unchanged despite the great inflation of the early sixteenth century. Even the most moderate fees could, of course, stretch the resources of the poor, but the impoverished were far less likely to be involved in instance litigation, the smallest estates were exempt from probate charges, and even fines imposed in office cases were sometimes pardoned for those whom the judges realised were unable to pay. Certainly it appears that fees did not act as a deterrent to quite ordinary people when they felt compelled to engage in matrimonial litigation (**48, 95, 103**).

It is difficult to determine how successful the courts were in the apprehension, conviction and punishment of sinners. Each court was concerned solely with the maintenance of order within its own jurisdiction; only in heresy cases is there evidence of communication between the authorities of different dioceses. The judicial procedure assumed fixed residence, and those who went to ground might avoid appearance before the judge. In the Canterbury consistory court in 1474 40 per cent of defendants failed to appear, and by the names of many cited in Suffolk in 1499 the registrar entered 'fled' or 'left'. The local community had effectively driven out its troublemakers, temporarily at least, but the souls of the sinners, unrepentant and uncorrected, were in jeopardy. Non-appearance was probably, however, no worse a problem for the ecclesiastical than for the royal courts, whose frequent sentences of outlawry were an admission of similar failure (**6, 94, 137**).

Those accused who did appear might be allowed to clear themselves by compurgation, that is, by producing in court a number of oath-helpers who would testify to their belief in the defendant's innocence. The logic of compurgation was that it provided a safeguard against malicious accusation by personal enemies, yet the person who had offended the whole community by anti-social behaviour had little hope of clearing himself in this way. Compurgation seems to have been little used in the higher courts, where more serious cases were heard; in the Lincoln audience court between 1514 and 1520 it was only undertaken in eight out of 160 cases, and in only two successfully. In the Buckinghamshire archdeaconry courts, however, it was attempted frequently and was usually successful. It was not, however, a mere formality; much depended on the skill of the judges, who appear to have discouraged the attempt when they had reason to think the defendant guilty. The system was, of course, open to abuse: the friends of the accused might share his guilt or be sympathetic to him. Few villagers, however, would probably have been prepared to risk the ecclesiastical penalties for perjury, let alone God's judgement. Compurgation appears to have worked less well in London, where it was apparently possible to find oath-helpers even when the guilt of the defendant was palpable. In England's village communities, on the other hand, the system could be a safeguard against vindictiveness while not serving to shelter serious transgressors (**6, 10, 95**).

As for the severity and effectiveness of punishment, the evidence is contradictory. There are strong indications that respectable Londoners in the early sixteenth century were disillusioned by the leniency shown to moral offenders and by the ease with which defamers and perjurers might escape the consequences of their actions. Yet the Commons in 1532 complained of the shame of open penance and of the rapacity of the courts in the imposition of monetary penalties. It has been suggested that the members feared the efficiency of the courts, either in the detection of heresy or in intrusion into their sexual lives (**10, 103**). The issue of heresy stands alone, because of the terrible consequences in cases of obduracy or relapse. In other matters, much depended on the social status and mental outlook of the offender. Penance was intended to be a spiritual medicine which would bring the sinner back to a state of grace, but it was also a symbol of reconciliation with the community and was intended as a deterrent to others. In most dioceses the discipline – the whipping of the offender around the churchyard – had fallen into disuse by the late fifteenth century and was only rarely used in serious cases. The normal penance was to go before the cross in the Sunday parish procession, clad only in a smock or shift, carrying a candle to be offered at the altar [**doc. 6**]. Sometimes the offender would be required to say a few words to discourage others from the same offence. Restitution was an essential part of penance, and in cases of defamation this entailed a public apology [**doc. 8**]. Increasingly in the early sixteenth century payment of a fine, earmarked for pious purposes, was permitted in lieu of public penance, especially to persons whose dignity and authority would be compromised. The richer offender had to pay more than his poorer neighbour; fines for fornication in London ranged from one shilling to £3 6s 8d. When penance was enforced, it was harsher for the recidivist than for the patently contrite sinner. It might cause dread, as in the case of a Buckinghamshire gentleman who in 1520 threatened suicide to avoid public shame – his penance was relaxed. Others with little status to be jeopardised may have easily shrugged off their temporary humiliation. All that can be said is that all the court records so far analysed suggest that ecclesiastical judges showed common sense, discretion and humanity in the imposition of punishment, taking regard for the sinner as an individual while endeavouring to maintain religious and social norms (**6, 35, 49, 94, 95**).

Most judges realised, however, that there were clear limits to their power, which depended on the attitudes of individuals, and even more of society as a whole. Excommunication, the ultimate sanction to force an accused person into court, would seriously inconvenience respectable members of society, because it rendered them incapable of pleading in secular courts and, in theory at least, cut them off from the commercial community. Pimps, prostitutes and others on the margins of society were unlikely to be affected by its practical or spiritual consequences. It was difficult to get them to court, and only in the case of heretics or subversives was it worth taking the ultimate step of enlisting the help of the king's officers to effect their capture. More serious, a shift in mental climate, such as that which apparently occurred in London in the early sixteenth century, when respectable citizens lost faith in the courts because of their supposed leniency, would render ecclesiastical justice almost superfluous, because it was irrelevant to the needs of society (**94, 95**).

The London experience, however, is exceptional. Elsewhere the instance business of the courts might fall away after 1500 as secular tribunals provided new remedies – and this decline was much more gradual in the north than in the south, and in the countryside than in the towns – but this was a matter of convenience rather than dissatisfaction with or resentment against ecclesiastical procedures. There was remarkably little hostility to the jurisdiction of the courts in matters of religious belief and practice, and of morality.

All those historians who in recent years have examined the records of individual courts, and those who have studied specific categories of business, have admired the conscientious discharge of their duties by all the court personnel, especially the judges. The early sixteenth-century Lincoln episcopal court book has been described as a record of 'intense and painstaking activity' (**6**, p. xxiii). In Canterbury diocese the impression gained from the act books of the immediate pre-Reformation period is that the higher officials of the courts regarded their occupations as a duty, not as an opportunity for profit (**94**). A comparative study of Norwich and Winchester dioceses has revealed that the courts promoted the security and stability of the matrimonial relationship, ensured that as far as possible the last wishes of the deceased were implemented, encouraged the termination of disputes by arbitration which would lead to a mutually acceptable settlement, and preserved equilibrium within local communities (**49**). All this was no small achievement. The late medieval English church courts consistently endeavoured to implement the high ideals of the universal canon law, and they did not deserve the opprobrium visited upon them, for political reasons, during the Reformation Parliament.

7 Religious Belief and Practice

The Mass and the Christian community

At the centre of the life of the medieval catholic church, and of the religious experience of all orthodox believers, stood the Mass, the daily repeated miracle by which the Body and Blood of Christ were created at the altar out of bread and wine [**doc. 7**]. In the late Middle Ages only the tiniest minority in England, as in the rest of Latin Christendom, gave any indication that they doubted that by this central ritual, performed only by priests, the entire Christian community shared in the grace of God.

The medieval Mass had two distinct elements. It was a sacrifice, performed by the priest on behalf of the community, a re-enactment of Christ's Passion by which He, at once God and man, had atoned for the sins of fallen mankind and provided the opportunity for salvation. It was also a sacrament in which the whole community participated, a memorial of the Last Supper with implications of social brotherhood. The role of the laity was limited, but they were not entirely passive, and perhaps the most significant aspect of their participation was the exchange, after the consecration by the priest of the Eucharist, of the sign of peace. A small board with a representation of Christ, known as the pax, was passed around the congregation and kissed by them in turn. Occasionally this led to sordid quarrels about precedence, but in general this ritual, together with the requirement that any person who took communion (which all were required to do once a year, at Easter) should be in a state of peace with his neighbours, served as a pacifying influence. It was hoped that the presence of Christ on the altar would bring peace to a society deeply divided, be it a parish torn by jealousy and feuds or a wider community. The consecrated Host, for example, was carried on Corpus Christi day in a resplendent procession through numerous English towns which were racked by internal faction, in the hope that universal and orderly participation in a civic ceremony in honour of the Body of Christ would bring unity and order to the social body. In

1459, indeed, a London riot was quelled by bishops bringing the Host into its midst. The Mass, therefore, stood at the centre not only of religious but of social life. It was the most potent weapon of the church in its constant campaign at all levels to impose harmony by arbitration and reconciliation (**32, 102, 107, 147**).

The centrality of the Mass to the religion and culture of the later Middle Ages is symptomatic of a shift of emphasis. Faith and observance became increasingly Christocentric. The new spirituality of the twelfth-century monasteries and cathedral schools, which had emphasised the friendship of the human Jesus rather than the wrath of the Old Testament patriarchal God, gradually captured the church at large. Concentration on the love of God manifest in Christ's Passion ensured that, in popular consciousness as much as among professional theologians, the sacrifice of the Mass would displace other, peripheral religious practices. This growing awareness of the significance of the Eucharist has been taken as a sign of the spiritual maturity of western Christianity. Attention throughout Latin Christendom was increasingly focused upon a single, central rite rather than upon the miracles of a multitude of localised saints (**111, 182**).

This popular preoccupation with the life and death of Christ, and by association with the Holy Family and most especially with His mother, had various manifestations. Shrines associated with Jesus and the Blessed Virgin Mary flourished as pilgrimage centres. The statue of the Virgin at Ipswich, the Holy Rood (or crucifix) of Bromholm and the Holy Blood of Hailes continued to attract visitors as the clientele of other shrines, such as that of Becket, apparently shrank (**42**). They provided comfort of a traditional kind, yet within the new devotional context, for those whose piety was more easily expressed by a physical rather than a mental journey. At the end of the fourteenth century Passion plays were greatly expanded within the cycles of mystery plays which covered the whole Bible story, a clear attempt to evoke feelings of compassion among those illiterate persons for whom drama was an important medium for the reception of the Christian message (**50, 122**). New devotions were introduced into the liturgy. The feast of the Name of Jesus achieved official recognition probably because of the enthusiasm of Henry VII's mother; new Marian festivals were introduced; and the feasts of the Five Wounds and the Crown of Thorns were further memorials of the Passion, which was depicted in increasingly realistic and horrific detail by sculptors and painters (**77**). This concentration on the suffering of Christ, at the expense of the Resurrection, has been regarded as excessively morbid and even spiritually unhealthy. In a world, however, in which agony was a common spectacle, in the form of painful disease unrelieved by effective medicine or of the dreadful executions inflicted on traitors and other felons, there must have been great comfort in the conviction that God had suffered with and for mankind and had thereby defeated the potent forces of evil and opened the pathway to eternal life for the faithful.

There developed a cult of the Eucharist, which found expression at many different levels. Meditation on the Passion and contemplation of the Host itself could lead to violent emotions. The extremes of grief and ecstasy revealed in the early fifteenth-century *Book of Margery Kempe* cannot have been unique to that East Anglian housewife (**5**). More common, however, was the imputation to the Host itself of magical qualities. That some more obvious manifestation of divine power was generally required than transubstantiation (which cannot, of course, be perceived by the eye) is attested by the appearance of collections of miracles of the Host which, just like the relics of saints, was alleged to have effected wonderful cures or to have visited retribution on those who did not show it proper respect. A sober pastoral manual stated that nobody would die on a day when they had attended Mass. It was popularly believed that a communicant who could carry away the consecrated Host in his mouth possessed an immense source of power which could be used for good or ill, even as a love charm (**89, 111**). A very different but nonetheless related phenomenon was the increasing habit from the late fourteenth century onwards among a very restricted section of the population of England – those of such status as allowed some privacy – of taking communion far more frequently in their domestic chapel or at a portable altar. This had some important implications. An obligation to communicate once a year was subtly transformed into a right to partake of the sacrament at will, in imitation of the practice of the priestly order and in contrast to the generality of laypeople; and private communion robbed the sacrament of its important social connotation (**40, 51, 111**).

That the laity were not alienated from the church and that they had the highest confidence in the efficacy of its central ritual is clearly indicated by the proliferation of votive masses, particularly those celebrated for the souls of the deceased, which supplemented and almost swamped the public or parish mass. Vast resources were invested by all classes of society, corporately or individually, in the endowment of intercessory masses to be celebrated at funerals and in sequences at various intervals thereafter, preferably until the end of the world, in chantry* chapels founded by the wealthy or at altars established by numerous confraternities.* The rationale is well expressed in a fourteenth-century foundation charter: 'Among other means of restoring fallen humanity, the solemn celebration of masses, in which for the well-being of the the living and the repose of the departed to God most high the Father His Son is offered, is to be judged highest in merit and of most power to draw down the mercy of God' (**185**, p. 48). King Henry VII left money for ten thousand masses to be celebrated within a month of his death, a magnificently lavish bequest, but merely an exaggerated manifestation of an aspiration common to most English people. It has been nicely suggested that 'never again, not even from Philip II's Spain, was the Almighty to endure such a barrage as he received from the unceasing soul masses of the chantry priests of late medieval England' (**172**, p. 102).

At the heart of this desperate desire for intercessory masses lay the doctrine of Purgatory, the belief, only precisely formulated in the late twelfth century, that there lay between Heaven and Hell an intermediate place, by passing through which the souls of the dead might cleanse themselves of the guilt attached to the sins committed during their lifetime by submitting to a graduated scale of divine punishments. Purgatory has often been regarded as an oppressive doctrine, symptomatic of the anxieties and uncertainties of the later Middle Ages. Yet as presented in the *Divine Comedy* of Dante Alighieri, a poetic genius who nevertheless expressed assumptions common to western Christians, it has been described as a 'place of hope, an initiation into joy, a gradual emergence into the light' (**60**, p. 346). Despite their torments, the souls in Purgatory were destined to be saved, in sharp contrast to those which would abide in Hell for all eternity. The suffering through which they were cleansed might, moreover, be abbreviated by the prayers of the living, and most especially by masses. The general commemoration of the souls of the faithful departed was hardly sufficient, for it was widely considered that the benefit accruing to the individual soul decreased in proportion to the number of the dead for whom prayers were offered. Countless testators therefore made provision for masses for their own souls, and to include kindred or associates as beneficiaries was an act of the greatest friendship. It is sad, if perhaps natural, that masses endowed in perpetuity by remote ancestors often tended to be neglected by their heirs as each generation made an ever-greater spiritual investment for the immediate kin-group (**31, 146**). Late medieval religion has been well described as 'a cult of living friends in the service of dead ones' (**102**, p. 42). The release of souls from Purgatory was the supreme act of charity, but it was charity which often remained very near home.

Although there are many earlier examples, it was in the fourteenth century that the endowment of a chantry*, a foundation whose main purpose was to provide daily or weekly masses for the benefit of named individuals, became the common aspiration of persons of wealth and status. The fashion started at the pinnacle of society; eighty-five aristocratic families in the fourteenth and fifteenth centuries, virtually all the higher nobility of England, established perpetual chantries, which were intended to survive until Doomsday (**81**). Many of these grandiose institutions centred on magnificent tombs, such as those of the bishops in Winchester Cathedral or of the earls in St Mary's, Warwick, while other founders converted an entire parish church into a college of chantry priests, as did Richard Duke of Gloucester in 1478 at Middleham. At the other end of the scale were innumerable simple altars established by members of the gentry and the merchant class in the side aisles of their local churches. Cheapest of all, Mass might be celebrated on a portable altar placed on top of the beneficiary's tomb (**79**).

The latest historian of the English chantries conducted a survey of twenty counties, containing half the parishes of England, and found therein 2182 chantries or similar institutions, each capable of supporting at least one priest. These figures do not include the numerous perpetual and temporary foundations established in monasteries, and hence underestimate the commitment of the English laity to intercessory masses (**31, 58**). There were regional variations. London, where there was a concentration of wealth, had 314 chantries in less than a hundred parish churches. In the north, one in two churches housed a chantry of some sort, while in no county of the south-east or midlands did this apply to more than one in five parishes. This is surely explained, however, by the far smaller geographical extent and greater concentration of parishes in the more populous areas. In short, the enthusiasm for chantry foundations was a national phenomenon, and it persisted into the sixteenth century (**58**). It is true that fewer perpetual chantries were established after 1450, and that there was a shift to temporary, if long-term, foundations. The reasons for this are several.

Founders perhaps realised that their more remote heirs were not certain to honour their intentions; 60 per cent of early fourteenth-century foundations in perpetuity had disappeared long before the Reformation. A temporary chantry and other pious bequests might be a better spiritual investment. It did not, moreover, require royal licence, as did the permanent alienation of lands to the church, and after 1450 this was becoming more difficult to obtain and more expensive (**31**). Economic contraction, too, was an obvious cause of the decline in perpetual foundations. A survey of the city of York has revealed that while severe urban decay prevented the citizens after 1450 from emulating their predecessors, who by then had established thirty-two perpetual chantries, the merchant class continued to endow as many prayers for their souls as they possibly could. Temporary chantries and the provision for lavish short-term commemoration by masses became the norm (**118**). In Lancashire, however, the foundation of chantries only reached its height after 1450: seven of the eleven in Manchester's church were established after 1498 (**58**). There is no sign of disillusionment or doubt that the celebration of masses hastened the arduous journey of the soul towards eternal beatitude.

Although intercession for the dead was the *raison d'être* of the chantries, their chaplains were also involved in improving the welfare of the living. In four sample counties, 8 per cent of them were engaged in some form of teaching, usually casual and poorly endowed, but they made a significant contribution to 'elementary' education. Even more crucial was their involvement in pastoral work. In these same four counties almost a quarter of the cantarists* were active in the cure of souls. Their work was vital in the large parishes of the north and in expanding towns such as Birmingham, Halifax and Doncaster, where the parochial structure of an earlier age had not adapted to later medieval shifts in population (**58**). Their service to the community was great, too, even in long-established centres. In fifteenth-century Bristol there were at least twenty perpetual chantries and 120 semi-permanent institutions, as well as a multitude of more ephemeral mass-endowments. Many of the chaplains rendered conspicuous assistance to the parish priests in all aspects of pastoral and liturgical life, and notably in the elaboration of parochial music. The general supervision by the mayor of their conduct was exercised as much for the benefit of living citizens as to safeguard the souls of the deceased (**108**). Detailed analysis of this important town has borne out the assertion that, for the majority of the English people, the dissolution of the chantries under Edward VI was of far greater consequence than the disappearance of the monasteries (**45**).

The desperate desire for intercessory masses, gratified for persons of substance by the chantries, was fulfilled for an infinitely larger number of English people by membership of confraternities or religious guilds. These voluntary associations existed throughout the medieval period, but they proliferated in England, as in the rest of western Europe, in the late fourteenth and fifteenth centuries. Membership varied according to the status of the confraternity and its function. The most prestigious, which held impressive ceremonial processions, attracted distinguished brethren from all over the country, including the court circle and the ecclesiastical hierarchy; such were the Holy Trinity Guild of Coventry and St Mary's Guild at Boston. The vast majority, however, were local associations, firmly based in the parish. It may be the case that in most market towns one dominant guild emerged whose membership was identical with the governing group, yet the majority of confraternities were not socially exclusive, although a different sort of limitation might be imposed by strict rules of moral conduct (**83, 136**). It is impossible to estimate at all accurately how many religious guilds there were in England as a whole. There appear to have been regional variations, but in London, the east of England and the midlands they were very thick on the ground. Over 150 have been identified in London and forty-five in Norwich (**31, 88**). There are strong indications that it was the fear of sudden death, indecent burial and oblivion in the wake of the Black Death which prompted many foundations, but the evidence of London wills suggests an increase rather than a decline in their popularity in the early sixteenth century, while 1176 persons enrolled in the great guild of Ludlow between 1505 and 1509 (**31, 83**).

At the heart of the confraternities lay deep lay devotion and a craving for mutual aid in the search for salvation. This spirit is well illustrated by the stated objectives of the Guild of Corpus Christi in the church of St Michael-on-the-Hill, Lincoln [**doc. 9**]. The most popular dedications of confraternities were to Corpus Christi, the Holy Trinity and the Blessed Virgin Mary; this reflects increasing lay preoccupation with the central tenets of the Christian faith, combined with a mounting tide of popular devotion to Mary, the supreme channel of intercession (**136, 170**). The corporate religious activity of this Lincoln guild, as of so many others, centred almost exclusively on veneration of the Eucharist, the dignity of which they wished to enhance as witness of their supreme confidence in its efficacy. The members of such groups could, for the most part, have afforded only very modest provision for masses in their own last testaments, but as brothers and sisters of the confraternity they became participators in the spiritual benefits which would accrue for all time to those whose names were entered in its register. There were, of course, advantages to be gained on this earth – such as the conviviality of the annual feast and the guarantee of mutual assistance. It was, however, the celestial dividend which attracted members, and even induced them to enrol their deceased relatives in the confraternities. If there was deep-seated fear of the pains of Purgatory, there was also almost universal confidence that the proliferation of masses would ease the pathway of the soul.

Piety and charity

It was alleged by a historian of Tudor philanthropy that charitable bequests by English people greatly increased in the century after 1540 due to theological changes and to the disappearance of religious houses and chantries; from around 1480, moreover, he detected 'pervasive secularism', with a decline in bequests which were purely religious and an increase in those directed towards social ends such as the alleviation of poverty and disease (**53**). His main conclusion, however, has been challenged because the statistics on which it is based take no account of the rampant inflation of the sixteenth century (**98**). In any case, it is impossible in the late medieval period to distinguish clearly between piety and charity (**180**). Very many bequests for intercessory prayer contained provision for distribution of alms to the poor, while hospitals and almshouses were religious institutions in which a continual round of prayer was maintained.

An index of the good works which were considered to confer spiritual benefit on the donor is provided by the indulgences* (limited to forty days' remission) granted by English bishops. Relatively few were granted for purely pious exercises, such as pilgrimages to the sites of miracles or prayers for a deceased individual. Many were given in return for contributions to churches which had suffered some great misfortune such as fire, and these were a charitable act to the congregations who would otherwise have to bear the cost of rebuilding. Just as many indulgences, however, were granted for causes which were not religious in any narrow sense:

the repair of roads and bridges, the support of deserving individuals impoverished by disease or injury, and the release of prisoners taken in the French war or by the Turks in the Eastern Mediterranean. Funds were raised by indulgences for hospitals, both local institutions and those of national reputation such as Bedlam, the London asylum for lunatics (**1**, **2**, **3**, **14**). The English bishops, therefore, made no clear distinction between piety and philanthropy when soliciting alms from the living, and it is certain that none existed in the minds of those who on their deathbed distributed their goods for the benefit of their souls [**doc. 10**].

The most obvious manifestation of the enthusiastic piety of late medieval England is the evidence provided by wills, churchwardens' accounts, and above all by surviving buildings, of the huge investment in parish churches, of which some six thousand surviving examples are built wholly or mainly in the Perpendicular style, which predominated from *c.* 1370 to the Reformation. In more prosperous regions saturation point had been reached by the end of the fifteenth century, but across the nation as a whole the energy and resources poured into the reconstruction and adornment of local churches was as great in the 1520s as a century earlier (**79**, **83**) [**doc. 1**] This architectural revolution was normally the result of concerted communal effort. At Eye (Suffolk) funds for building the magnificent church tower were raised in a year from regular income, church-ales* and legacies, but mostly from the gifts of numerous living parishioners. In 1527 All Hallows-on-the-Wall in London was rebuilt, partly by the profits of a parish play, but mostly by subscription. Even when one family took the lead, as did the Cloptons at Long Melford (Suffolk), it merely prompted and orchestrated an effort by the whole community of the parish (**64**, **79**, **180**). Examples could be multiplied almost infinitely from all over England. Here at least is a clear indication that the vast majority of parishioners identified whole-heartedly with their own local church.

It has been alleged that wills cannot be used as an indication of testators' religious convictions, because the proximity of death might be an incentive to piety which had not been manifested in life. This assertion is countered by the multitude of gifts made by the living to the fabric of parish churches. It has also been argued that the parish priest, so often the scribe, might influence deathbed bequests. There is no reason, however, why an incumbent or a curate should have encouraged legacies to neighbouring churches as well as to his own, or to religious houses or to the friars.

Certainly the approach of death may have concentrated the mind on the spiritual benefits of generous giving, for according to the oft-quoted Biblical text, 'Alms extinguish sin as water does fire' (Ecclesiasticus, 3, 33); but the precise distribution of that third part of the testator's movables traditionally set aside to be used for the good of his soul was surely a matter of personal choice.

Late medieval wills, which survive in vast numbers, confirm this grea and overriding commitment to parish churches [**doc. 10**]. Of lay testators in Norwich between 1370 and 1532, 95 per cent made bequests to their parish church, and 90 per cent of early sixteenth-century Suffolk wills make similar provision (**64**, **88**). A more general survey has led to the conclusion that in the decades before the Reformation legacies in money and kind were pouring into the parishes (**83**). These ranged from innumerable small donations, for the provision of lights around the altar or at shrines, to major benefactions for the rebuilding of belfries made by the gentry, whose religious lives had come to centre on the parish churches on their estates rather than on monastic or mendicant houses, as in earlier centuries. In Gloucestershire, Kent and Yorkshire the great majority of this class sought burial in parish churches, which were often enough dominated by their tombs or chantry chapels (**91**, **127**, **172**). The members of urban oligarchies similarly resorted in death to the most prominent parish church of their town, so that at Hull 'Holy Trinity in particular must have seemed like a Council Chamber of deceased civic officers and their wives' (**40**, p. 215). Great city churches like St Mary Redcliffe in Bristol and St Peter Mancroft in Norwich were built on a grand scale to the greater glory both of God and of prosperous merchant communities, and as centres for civic as well as religious ritual.

Despite this overwhelming generosity to parish churches, the decline in donations to the religious orders should not be overestimated. Approximately 40 per cent of London wills between 1370 and 1530 contain some bequest to the regulars*, and there is little sign of lessening enthusiasm towards the end (**180**). A large random sample of English last testaments of the early sixteenth century reveals that one in six included deathbed bequests to the enclosed orders and one in five to the friars (**83**). Despite their literary image, the mendicant orders certainly appear to have maintained their popularity, especially among the more prosperous classes who had resources to spare after demonstrating devotion to their parish church. They were extensively patronised by the gentry and the burgesses of London and provincial towns (**40**, **91**,

127, **180**). The monks and canons were less popular, but the decline in giving is only relative. In earlier centuries the monasteries had received extensive grants of land which had consolidated their position as landowners. Such lavishly endowed corporations were unlikely now to appear as deserving causes. But bequests were still made in fairly large numbers to small, impoverished communities, and more particularly to the nunneries (**91**). The most significant fact, however, is that houses which were known to be austere and devoted to spiritual excellence continued to attract gifts. Syon and Sheen near London and the northern charterhouses of Mount Grace and Beauvale – all centres of forms of devotion relevant to the laity – were well supported (**91, 127, 180**). There is every indication that those people with sufficient resources to make a will were becoming highly selective in their attitude to the religious.

This same discrimination was increasingly shown in bequests for the relief of the poor, sick and aged. From the mid-fifteenth century it became more common to append to a chantry foundation some institution of social utility, such as an almshouse, hospital or school (**132**). This tendency contributes to the impression that there was an increase in philanthropy at the end of the Middle Ages. Charity was not, however, dispensed unconditionally, as it had perhaps been in the age of St Francis, when the poor were viewed as the image of Jesus and riches were not considered a manifestation of moral superiority (**82**). Just as the relationship between the testator and the priest employed for the celebration of masses was contractual, so too was that with the poor who, in return for relief, were expected to offer their less efficacious, but still valuable, prayers for the soul of their benefactor. The statutes of Croydon almshouse, established in 1447, required the seven poor inmates to say specified prayers each day in the parish church, and after the founder's death to pray around his tomb (**14**). In addition to the huge number of masses endowed for his soul, Henry VII expected prayers from the hundred poor men sheltered, on a nightly basis, in his new hospital of the Savoy. Poor persons who were incited to attend the funerals of the great by the promise of a dole were summoned perhaps partly out of compassion for their state, but more for the honour rendered to the deceased and his kin by a large congregation at his obsequies, and most of all for the multiplication of prayers which could be achieved at relatively low cost (**82, 91**).

There was, moreover, an increasingly frequent insistence in wills that the poor who benefited therefrom should be worthy. A clear distinction emerged in the fifteenth century between deserving and undeserving poor, and this was enshrined in the post-Reformation Tudor poor law. This differentiation probably arose because of the post-plague rise in wages and the relative decline in the prosperity of those who, nevertheless, still had a surplus to expend in alms. There was a general move to restrict charity to specified groups or individuals who were suffering through no fault of their own, respectable and productive members of society who had fallen on hard times, and to exclude those who appeared to their social betters to be feckless idlers and parasites. This trend can be seen in Cambridge throughout the fifteenth century and in Yorkshire from about 1450 (**82**, **91**). If economic resentment led to the rejection of the 'sturdy beggar', the increasing lay preoccupation with morality which may be discerned in the attitudes of Henry VI and of the aldermen of London led to insistence on chastity and sobriety as essential qualifications for the receipt of charity. The relief of poverty and of suffering was becoming increasingly regulated and controlled, and the economic reasons for this corrective element in almsgiving were perhaps disguised in the minds of benefactors by the demands of their moralistic piety. The discretion of the clergy in the distribution of alms was gradually reduced as administration was entrusted by testators to town corporations or trade guilds, groups who could be guaranteed to share their own prejudices (**82**).

Lay initiative and the problem of anticlericalism

All over western Europe in the later Middle Ages laypeople increasingly took the initiative in the direction of religion. They did not reject the doctrine and forms which had been devised by the priesthood, but rather adapted and even amplified them to suit their own needs. It was, after all, the laity who financed the endless multiplication of masses for the dead. The proliferation of prayer was not imposed on the people by avaricious clergy, but rather priests responded to consumer demand. Benefactors, during their lives or on their deathbeds, were free to choose the recipients of their donations; gifts might be solicited, they could not be demanded. The initiative for the reallocation of resources from monasteries to parish churches and hospitals came from the laity; popes and bishops accepted, rather than instigated, this redistribution (**120**).

Power and wealth allowed great latitude in the choice of religious forms. The spiritual climate of the English royal court in the late fourteenth century was influenced far more by the captains of the Hundred Years War than by bishops or chaplains (**109**). A foundress such as Margaret, Lady Hungerford (d. 1478) quite clearly expressed her own religious preferences and convictions in the design of her chantry chapel and in the liturgical forms to be used therein (**146**). Funeral directions might provide for lavish pomp or utmost austerity. Despite the association of simplicity in burial with Lollard sympathies, it is quite certain that both extremes were requested by those of unassailable orthodoxy and that the clergy fulfilled the variant wishes of the deceased (**91, 127**).

The laity also exercised great control over the employment of priests. The patronage of many parish churches remained in the hands of lay lords and an increasing number of clergy were engaged by laymen to serve as the chaplains of temporary chantries or of confraternities. Church livings were used extensively to provide for the younger sons of gentry families, but there is evidence that some patrons, such as the Courtenay Earls of Devon, did seek to support promising young men of the locality in the first stages of their careers (**124**). There seems to have been increasing lay concern for the quality of the priesthood. Lord Grey, touring his Welsh estates in the 1440s, embarked on a personal campaign to enforce celibacy. The civil authorities of London expelled scandalous priests from the city, and many wills stipulated that the priest employed to celebrate soul masses should be chaste and worthy (**31, 91, 95**).

Within the parish community, too, the laity took increasing responsibility for their own affairs. This initiative was not usurped, but rather was encouraged by the ecclesiastical authorities. By the late fourteenth century bishops had accepted that parishioners, represented by their churchwardens, who were chosen from the respectable element amongst them, were suitable custodians of church property, most of which had been provided by lay contribution (**158**). It was the obligation of the churchwardens as much as of the incumbent priest to enforce the social norms of Christianity, and this extended to the duty of denouncing during visitation the shortcomings of the local clergy. In matters of discipline as of observance, responsible laymen acted in partnership with the ecclesiastical authorities. The laity had recovered much of the influence which had been lost in the twelfth century in the wake of the papal reform movement. The church hierarchy fostered this renewed initiative because it had succeeded so well in transmitting to some at least of the laity a knowledge of Christian doctrine and observance which would have been unimaginable in the early Middle Ages. The reforming ideal now embraced the laity, rather than being directed against them.

Increased lay activity does not imply dissatisfaction with the priesthood. The impression that there was widespread anticlericalism in late medieval England is fostered by the volume of satire and complaint against the clergy. It is salutary to remember that many identifiable authors of such polemic, and all the preachers who thundered from their pulpits, were themselves clerics, and that their anger was directed against those of their order who tarnished the priestly image (**75, 84**). It would be dangerous to conclude that such impassioned pleas for the purification of the English clergy constituted an attack on the clerical order as a whole. It has, indeed, been suggested that violent anticlericalism is only provoked by aggressive clericalism, such as that practised by the Teutonic Knights in contemporary Prussia (**31**). Such assertive solidarity was not manifested in England, where so much critical analysis of failings proceeded from the ranks of the clergy.

It has recently been claimed that the term 'anticlericalism' is a 'convenient fiction', based on 'an embarrassingly narrow range of examples' (**131**, pp. 391–2). Polemical attacks on Wolsey, it is convincingly argued, were directed from the camp of his political enemies. Wealthy clerics attracted hostility because they were wealthy, not because they were clerics. The much exaggerated anticlericalism of the Reformation Parliament was stage-managed by Thomas Cromwell for his own ends. Complaints against clergy during visitation were remarkably infrequent, and this clearly indicates that responsible provincial society was at least passively satisfied with the ministrations of local pastors (see pages 48–51). Positive evidence of general lay sympathy for the priesthood is provided by the high level of ordinations in the early sixteenth century and by continuing generous benefactions (**131**).

Fees and mandatory offerings due to the church have conventionally been considered a major cause of anticlericalism, but examination of the records does not substantiate this view. Probate fees were not extortionate and bore relatively heavily only on those merchants who had little land but much movable wealth (see page 59). Despite the notorious case of Richard Hunne, entirely exceptional both because of the attitude of the man and the fierce reaction of the ecclesiastical authorities, there were few mortuary disputes – only six, for example, in the large diocese of Norwich between 1519 and 1529 (**49**). The poor appear to have been exempt from this payment, and it would have been strange had there been widespread resistance when the majority of testators voluntarily gave more to the church in their last testaments.

The most burdensome payment, regular and uniform, was tithe – the tenth of produce or income due to the church. Tithe disputes were fought out in the courts, but they affected few parishes – ten out of 650 in Coventry and Lichfield diocese in 1525, and ten out of 1148 in Norwich in 1529. Most disputes concerned not the principle, which was almost universally accepted, but the rate at which tithes should be paid. Since the system had been devised for an agrarian society, this was a delicate problem in commercial centres, particularly London, where a complicated formula based on the rental value of property had been adopted; in such circumstances it is not surprising that there should have been misunderstandings and some subterfuge (**95, 106, 179**). In rural England disputes as to the ownership of tithes caused more litigation than refusal to pay. In those few cases where there was objection to payment, it was normally because tithes were used outside the parish by a monastic house to which the church was appropriated*, or because the recipient was plainly unworthy. It is easy to understand the indignation, for example, of the Norfolk parishioners whose parson allegedly collected his tithes with his mistress riding pillion on his saddle (**46, 49**). Such isolated instances do not, however, demonstrate general resistance to tithes or anticlerical sentiments (**131**).

There are certainly cases of lay resentment of individual unworthy or tactless priests which, when accumulated, give an impression of widespread discontent with the clergy as an order, but this, view is dispelled when it is remembered how small was the proportion of parishes troubled by such grievances in every diocese whose records have been analysed, and that legitimate complaints were normally dealt with swiftly by the ecclesiastical authorities, and were therefore short-lived. There were small groups in whose interests it was to encourage anticlerical sentiments – the common lawyers who resented loss of fees to the church courts, the political faction opposed to Wolsey. They were influential, vocal and articulate, but their views did not reflect those of the vast majority of the English people.

The Lollard challenge

In the late fourteenth century, for the first time in England, the doctrines and practices of the Catholic church were challenged and repudiated by a group of heretics who were dubbed 'Lollards' by the orthodox. Their creed was based on the writings of the Oxford don John Wyclif (d. 1384), a philosopher and theologian of some distinction, who was profoundly concerned by the failings of the contemporary church. His bitter criticism of the Papacy and his advocacy of reform by the lay power attracted powerful support at a time of English disillusionment with the Avignon popes and horror at the outbreak of the Great Schism. Wyclif, however, although forced by the contemporary situation to deal with matters of church government, was no politician, but a committed evangelical reformer who reached two conclusions, both firmly based on the logic of his own philosophy and his reverence for the Bible as 'the mirror of eternal truth': that all human beings are predestined either to salvation or to damnation, and that therefore their own actions, however meritorious they may appear, cannot affect their fate; and that the bread and wine of the Mass are not annihilated and transformed into the Body and Blood of Christ. He did not devalue the Eucharist, but rather held that its significance had been perverted. It was blasphemous to hold that priests, many of them predestined to damnation, could create Christ's Body. Christ's presence at the Mass was sacramental and spiritual – the result of God's promise to the faithful, not of the priest's words. Wyclif, in short, wished to dissociate the Eucharist from what he saw as superfluous and harmful manifestations of popular religion, such as pilgrimages and images, which were not sanctioned by the Scriptures, and most of all he decried the tendency to venerate the Host as if it were God (**55**, **111**).

In this, Wyclif had points of contact with contemporary orthodox theologians, but his tendency to push his arguments to the logical extreme with no regard for tradition or common usage led to the loss of governmental patronage as well as to ecclesiastical condemnation [**doc. 12a**]. It is remarkable, nevertheless, how much support his ideas attracted in the thirty years after his death. Despite assiduous propaganda that his teaching lay behind the Peasants' Revolt of 1381, and notwithstanding the introduction in 1401 of the death penalty for heresy, it is clear that Lollardy was not eliminated at Oxford, that Wyclif's views were widely disseminated outside the university, and that they were attractive not only to country priests and artisans but also to a group of knights within the royal court circle (**55, 65**). An academic heresy had developed into a broadly-based popular movement.

This transplantation from the lecture-room to the world was not characterised by any immediate degeneration. The arguments of the early Lollards were generally coherent and their evangelical methods sophisticated (**30, 50**). The leaders realised the importance of preaching and the provision of texts in the vernacular. Innumerable writings appeared – handbills listing abbreviated proposals for reform, short tracts, translations of the Bible or parts thereof, and perhaps most impressive, a formidable collection of 294 sermons. That this collection exists in thirty-one surviving manuscripts which were carefully collated with a common exemplar indicates considerable academic rigour and efficient organisation (**50**). The Lollard disendowment bill, probably of 1410, reveals considerable acumen in advancing proposals for the radical reorganisation of the church: confiscation of the property of the religious orders could benefit every element of English society, from a newly-created aristocracy and squirearchy through the students of fifteen new universities and fifteen thousand adequately endowed priests to the infirm occupants of a hundred new almshouses (**40**). The ecclesiastical authorities in the early fifteenth century had every justification for their fear of the sect.

Lollardy, however, did not succeed in establishing itself as a national religion, as did the broadly similar Hussite faith in contemporary Bohemia. Many factors contributed to this failure. The desire of the aristocracy to appropriate church lands was tempered by fear of Lollard sedition. The radical element within the church, notably the friars, who had initially agreed with many of Wyclif's proposals, had been alienated by his denial of transubstantiation. Orthodox theologians had at an early stage mounted an intellectual and spiritual counter-attack, and the failure of the church to cater for lay demand for vernacular religious texts has been much exaggerated (see page 83). It may be that Lollardy, while attacking the validity of much contemporary belief and practice, failed to provide satisfying alternatives; most particularly, and inevitably because of Wyclif's predestinarianism, it denied any means by which a Christian might contribute by his own efforts to his salvation.

The main reason for the failure of Lollardy was, however, perhaps political. Despite his confidence in the secular power as an agent of reform, Wyclif lost the support of the crown, whereas the Bohemian monarchy fostered a native movement of religious dissent as an agent of its own aggrandisement (**183**). It was royal acquiescence, and subsequently the king's active support, which enabled the ecclesiastical authorities to conduct a vigorous campaign to eradicate the sect. It was probably desperation which led to the abortive Lollard uprising of 1414 led by Sir John Oldcastle. This merely confirmed what the church had always argued, that heresy and sedition were inextricably interrelated. The defeat by Henry V of this pathetic rebellion marked a cross-roads not only for the followers of Wyclif, but for the English church as a whole (**110**).

Lollardy was now driven underground. A few inspired itinerant preachers, such as Wiliam White in East Anglia in the 1420s, managed for a while to maintain some coherence of belief. Minor insurrections in the 1430s revealed some vestigial organisation (**30, 90**). Books continued to circulate within, even between, local groups, and the possession of such writings was for the authorities the surest test of heretical depravity; there was, however, no new literary production after the early fifteenth century. Thereafter the intellectual rigour of early Lollardy was lost, opinions varied even within groupings, and it is probably more accurate to describe the beliefs of the heretics rather 'as a set of more or less consistent attitudes than as a set of carefully worked-out doctrines' (**90**, p. 239).

The main and constant strands of the heresy are, however, well illustrated by the abjuration of a Herefordshire Lollard in 1505 [**doc. 12b**]. The possessor of forbidden books, he had openly declared against transubstantiation, confession to priests, penance and the veneration of images. He was anti-papal, considering the Bishop of Rome to be Antichrist, and also, which was less common, he repudiated the sacrament of matrimony. The same attitudes are revealed in the confessions of a group from the Newbury area of Berkshire between 1488 and 1491, some of whom expressed violently anti-sacerdotal views and a contempt for church buildings (**29**). The underlying themes of late Lollard belief were scriptural fundamentalism and common-sense rationalism. The first is typified by the rejection of images because of the second commandment given to Moses; the second by the assertion that only fools go on pilgrimage to Compostella, and that money is much better spent at home on the relief of the poor. Transubstantiation was denied on both scores, although some Lollards did view the Mass as a commemoration of Christ's redemption of mankind.

Analysis

A listing of heresy cases between 1414 and 1520 gives the initial impression that the sect had many adherents; yet over the century remarkably few parishes were involved. The north of England was almost totally immune from heresy until the importation of Lutheran influences (**90**). There were certain pockets of endemic Lollardy in groups of parishes in Berkshire, Essex and Kent. It has been calculated that in the 1520s a quarter of three hundred persons listed for tax purposes in 1524 in four south Buckinghamshire parishes can be described as Lollards or sympathisers, and that some of these were substantial property-owners. Similarly the Coventry group of 1511–12 contained a wide cross-section of more prosperous artisans (**126**, **168**). These were, however, exceptional areas. The complete orthodoxy of wills from Eton, close by the Lollard strongholds, shows how very localised was the heresy, and very few wills from the country as a whole reveal any affinity with heretical beliefs (**159**, **172**). There is evidence of some communication between the various groups in the early sixteenth century, largely through journeymen in the textile industry, and this network proved useful for the circulation of Protestant books in the 1520s, when contact was established between the old heretics and the new (**38**). Before this, however, the travellers had not evangelised outside known centres of their faith. Lollardy was essentially a family religion, fostered to a remarkable degree by women and practised within extended households mainly in certain small and clearly defined areas of the country (**30**).

It has often been suggested that the hierarchy overreacted in its persecution of Lollardy, but in the light of their knowledge of events in contemporary Bohemia, this accusation is hardly justified (**110**). The records of the trials suggest that the judges made every effort to establish the truth rather than merely to convict on suspicion. The procedures of the Inquisition, including the use of torture, were never introduced to England. The courts did everything possible to convince the accused of the errors demonstrable in their beliefs, and the invocation of the secular arm to execute the offender was used only as a last resort, for it was an admission of failure (**90**). The proportion of burnings to prosecutions is very small; in 1521 Bishop Longland rounded up three to four hundred heretics in Buckinghamshire, but only four were executed (**34**). While excessive caution on the part of the ecclesiastical authorities resulted in court appearances for many who were crudely superstitious or deranged, it is certain that only those who persisted in heresy or who relapsed after abjuration were delivered to the stake.

The humane historian may deprecate any form of religious persecution, although the record of twentieth-century man hardly permits the passing of moral judgements on previous generations. It must, however, be allowed that if on the eve of the Reformation Lollardy was an irritant rather than a real danger, this was due to firm action by generations of English bishops.

The implications of literacy

The true extent of the expansion of lay literacy in late medieval England has only recently been appreciated. A survey of educational provision in York diocese, which contained 10 per cent of the nation's population spread over a wide area traditionally considered backward, has revealed the existence of 250 schools of various sorts during the two centuries before the Reformation. This total is equal to the previous highest estimate for the whole country. Not all were permanent, and some were very small, but they nevertheless offered educational opportunities far greater and far lower down the social scale than historians have hitherto imagined (**68**). Most boys were doubtless sent to school for practical reasons, for an increasing number of careers required literacy. The ability to read, however, inevitably affected attitudes to religion.

The early medieval church had been geared to a world in which literacy was the preserve of a tiny minority, mostly clerics. The main means of religious instruction were visual and dramatic. The orthodox response to the needs of the increasing numbers of literate laity, however, predated the impact of Lollardy: it was not merely a defence mechanism devised to combat the threat of a vernacular heresy. From the mid-fourteenth century at the latest, numerous writers, with the encouragement of the episcopate, produced a multitude of works in English designed to introduce literate Christians to the central doctrines of their faith. These covered a wide spectrum, from rudimentary instruction to elaborate devotional treatises (**76**). The provision of this literature has been seen as a direct rebuttal of the charge that the church was unresponsive to the shifting needs of the laity (**120**), and if, as has been suggested, literacy distanced its practitioners from traditional procedures and institutions (**30**), this was not because of any myopic failure by the ecclesiastical authorities to appreciate that religious literature should be freely available.

Such works were shaped by monastic values, adapted to suit the needs of those who wished to live a religious life while remaining in the world; 'owing to the expansion of devout literature in the later Middle Ages, a larger public than ever before came to share in the spiritual treasure won in monastic solitude' (**96**, p. 149). The two most popular and influential texts, both written in the north in the late fourteenth century, were Walter Hilton's *The Scale of Perfection*, and the *Mirror of the Blessed Lyfe of Jesu Crist*, translated by the Carthusian Nicholas Love (**51**, **76**). *The Scale* (Latin *scala* = ladder) emphasised that it was possible for laypeople, without abandoning their public and social responsibilities, to climb nearer to God through their own spiritual endeavours. Contemplation of the divine was not the prerogative of the enclosed religious. The *Mirror* was at once a book of spiritual guidance and a translation of the synopsis of the Gospels; its availability did much to compensate for the ban on an English Bible imposed to counter the Lollard threat.

The continuing popularity of these works is indicated by the fact that between 1486 and 1533 *The Scale* was printed five times and the *Mirror* achieved nine impressions (**51**). Orthodox religious works, indeed, poured off the presses from the late fifteenth century, and the printing houses, even if influenced by powerful patrons such as the Lady Margaret Beaufort, were primarily seeking to make a profit by satisfying popular demand. Fifteenth-century wills reveal a steady increase in lay ownership of popular liturgical and devotional works, and it appears that these were the staple reading matter of the literate laity. By 1500 a very large number of lay people must have had an understanding of the faith which a century and a half before would have been restricted to the better educated among the clergy (**68**).

One of the dominant themes of this voluminous literature was the exhortation to the Christian to ponder deeply his personal relationship with God. The emphasis first placed by the great monastic theologians of the twelfth century on love and friendship between God and the individual was now transmitted to a wider lay audience (**69**). One important consequence was a shift in the interpretation of the role of confession. In the early Middle Ages its prime function had been to reconcile the sinner with the church and the community. From the twelfth century theologians had concentrated more on personal feelings of guilt and on release therefrom by the re-establishment of interior peace with God. In theory annual confession, made obligatory for all Christians by the Fourth Lateran Council of 1215, was private; in practice the rest of the parish, including the penitent's enemies, would be standing around in church, although probably out of earshot. For the vast majority of laypeople, and probably for most parish priests, confession remained a ritual of social pacification and reconciliation. Absolution could not be granted if the penitent intended to remain in a state of hostility with his neighbours. Amends had to be made, and penance was graduated according to the disruption which it had caused within the community (**100**, **121**) [**doc. 8**].

The confessional manuals produced in the later Middle Ages emphasised that the priest should strive to maintain social harmony through confession, but also urged that he should educate the conscience of the penitent, inducing him in turn to feelings of deep guilt and to the relief experienced through full reconciliation with God. Genuine remorse was more likely to be stimulated by confession that was truly private (**51**). By the fourteenth century all the English aristocracy had their personal confessors. The results of this intimate relationship between priest and sinner, which encouraged self-analysis, can be seen in the 'penitential rhetoric' in which Edward III's military commanders cast their wills, and most especially in a remarkable spiritual treatise, the *Livre de Seyntz Medicines*, written by Henry Duke of Lancaster, which is a heartfelt and extended personal confession, made vivid by the concerted use of military and medical metaphors (**76**, **109**).

The practice of private confession gradually filtered down the social scale to others influenced by the new style of devotional literature. Hilton in *The Scale* asserted that annual confession in the parish church was a social necessity, but believed that it could not satisfy the needs of the devout, who required frequent dialogue with a sympathetic confessor who could lead them through true contrition to the re-establishment of a loving relationship with God (**17**, **51**). The instructions compiled for a devout layman in the early fifteenth century, probably by his confessor, emphasised that he should end each day with a searching examination of his conscience (**165**). Such constant introspection surely made frequent private confession a psychological necessity. In the fifteenth century also, pastoral theologians began to argue that sin was something which occurred in the mind and that, as Peter Abelard had asserted three hundred years before, God took account of intention rather than consequence; thus lecherous thoughts began to be considered a serious sin, even if they did not culminate in promiscuity (**100**). It is probable that only a small minority even of the literate laity of pre-Reformation England experienced such deep feelings of guilt or, paradoxically, through combatting their sinful inclinations felt such a sense of spiritual worth. Those who did, however, came from the upper levels of society, and their deep and personal religious experience surely served to divorce them from popular belief and rites.

There were other, more tangible, manifestations of the interiorisation or 'privatisation' of religion among the upper classes (**40**). There seems to have been a great increase in the habit of private prayer, detached from the liturgical cycle of the church. By 1500 primers – prayer books intended for personal use – were among the most common books mentioned in lay wills (**30**). The religion of the nobility, gentry and upper stratum of the merchant class came increasingly to be centred on the household; Sir Thomas More's was exceptional only because of the intellectual capacity of its master. The trend had begun in the late fourteenth century in the chapels of the aristocracy, which reflected private taste in decoration and vestments (**109**). The practice of setting aside a room for prayer percolated down to a level less elevated but still highly respectable; between 1370 and 1458 the bishops of Exeter issued 903 licences for private oratories, and the Papacy granted numerous indults for the use of a portable altar, the real attraction of which was the facility to have Mass celebrated within the household (**7, 128**). Indeed, exceptionally devout individuals might transform their houses into what were in effect little churches, whose regime was based on the monastic programme adapted to lay usage [**doc. 11**]. In one early fifteenth-century household a devotional work would be passed round to be read by the diners in turn, and afterwards there would be edifying talk over the table (**165**). The religious miscellany compiled by a Yorkshire gentleman in mid-century contains constant reminders of the obligation to fulfil conscientiously social duties incumbent on one in his position, with the clear implication that these were a burdensome distraction from the pursuit of holiness within the household (**150**). The model for this was provided by the extended Holy Family, the sparse accounts of which in the Gospels were supplemented by apocryphal stories and which, it has been suggested, filled a similar role as an exemplum of domestic conduct to that of the royal family today (**32, 41**). The wide and continuing popularity of this ideal of familial religion is demonstrated by the wide circulation in the 1530s of *The Work for Householders* by Richard Whitford, a dialogue between master and household designed to strengthen devotion within the home (**76**). The domestic religion of late medieval England emphasised the puritanical element within Christianity, which is not to say that it deviated in the slightest from orthodoxy. If popular religion may be seen as a battle between Carnival and Lent, a balance of feast and fast, within the pious family unit it was the ascetic strain which predominated.

While much of the religious life of the social elite in the century and a half before the Reformation was conducted in private, even when they emerged into public view they tended to be increasingly isolated, physically and perhaps mentally, from the generality of Christians (**40**). In parish churches there was a great proliferation of side chapels in which the families which had endowed them might hear Mass apart from the local community, and in the nave of the church the introduction of private pews, reserved for the well-to-do, created a gulf between them and their plebeian neighbours. Seated thereon, respectable families, distinguished both by social status and by literacy, might follow the Mass in an English exposition or recite the Rosary, an increasingly popular form of devotion which symbolised the desire for a personal relationship with the Blessed Virgin Mary [**doc. 1**]. Confident of their superiority, those who exercised the local government and controlled the economic assets of late medieval England can scarcely have been unaware, even if they gave the matter little thought, of the divide in religious culture which had opened between them and the mass of the people.

A plurality of religious forms

Among a small sector of the population of England, as of western Europe as a whole, there had been a subtle shift of emphasis. Individual expressions of piety assumed a greater significance than participation in public religious ceremonies. From amongst that minority who were both literate and had some access to privacy, some devout persons had come to appreciate the implications of that great theological advance of the twelfth century whereby the tribal God of the early Middle Ages, who worked great magic for His people, had been transformed into a deity who operated secretly in the hearts of believers.

The vast majority, however, remained untouched by this change in mental climate. Ritual still stood at the heart of parish life. The festivals and fasts of the church corresponded to and marked out the passage of the agrarian year. There was as much need in the early sixteenth century as in the tenth for the supernatural aid of

God, dispensed through the church. Church bells were consecrated so that by their ringing storms might be averted, and formal curses were fulminated against pests and weeds in the cornfield. The distinction that these were sacramentals, effective only if God so willed, rather than magical spells, was surely beyond the comprehension of most parishioners (**89**). Shrines associated with Christ and His Mother no doubt attracted some pilgrims because they evoked sentiments of pity and compassion which had been engendered by devotional reading. But many more must have flocked to them because they now appeared to be offering the most effective form of curative magic, miracles of the traditional kind, such as that which was reported at Ipswich in 1515 (**64**). Some caution and reflection is advisable before religious beliefs and practices which satisfied the needs and aspirations of the vast majority of the population of late medieval England are decried as superstitious, and therefore inferior.

The gulf between the two religions of late medieval England can, indeed, be exaggerated. If the women of Kirkstall borrowed the girdle of St Bernard from the local abbey to wear during their confinements, so too Henry VII's wife hired a girdle of Our Lady to safeguard her in her pregnancy (**89**). Relics were still prized, if increasingly now accumulated in private collections rather than deposited in religious houses for the common good (**40**). Devotional writers might consider them valuable as aids to contemplation, but it would be dangerous to assume that their owners did not expect them to give protection and work wonders, as they had in a previous age. If printers flooded the market with works intended to foster meditation on Christ's life, there were excellent sales too for the *Golden Legend*, a comprehensive collection of the deeds of saints. Manifestations of the new interior piety could coexist easily with ostentatious displays of public religion, as in the reburial of Richard Duke of York in 1476 (**96**). The prevalence of traditional forms of religion at the apex of society is well illustrated by the actions of Anthony, Lord Rivers, who went on pilgrimage to Rome, obtained there an indulgence for the chapel at Westminster rebuilt by his father [**doc. 4a**], and in his will of 1483 left his body to Our Lady of Pontefract, his heart to Our Lady of the Pew and his hair shirt to Our Lady of Doncaster (**41**). Only his devotion to Mary perhaps distinguishes his piety from that of the nobility of the twelfth century. That a wide variety of religious forms could appeal to one person is nowhere better illustrated than in the commonplace book of Robert Reynys, churchwarden of Acle in Norfolk (d. 1474). It contains English summaries of basic religious knowledge such as the Ten Commandments, the Seven Deadly Sins and the Seven Sacraments; a prose account of the life of St Bridget and verses on the Rosary – both aspects of the new devotion of the later Middle Ages; an apocryphal papal indulgence for those who carried the length of the nails used at the crucifixion 'and worship them daily with 5 *Paternosters* and 5 *Aves* and a psalter'; numerous charms against dangers and sickness, and one for conjuring up angels (**155**). Literacy did not always give birth to inordinate sophistication which cut off its possessors from the common assumptions of the populace.

The new informed and 'interiorised' piety could itself take different forms. King Henry VI was presented by his biographer, and has generally been taken, as the model of the devout late medieval English layman. He was profoundly occupied by the Passion and by the Real Presence in the Mass. He read the Bible in English and engaged in regular private prayer. He enforced observance of the Sabbath on his court and was puritanical to the point of prudishness. His concern for his soul led to the foundation of two great chantry chapels, Eton and King's College, Cambridge, which were to develop into notable educational establishments. Yet this preoccupation with personal salvation, this turning away from the world and its concerns, was perhaps a contributory factor in his disastrous record as king. Henry's piety has been characterised as self-regarding and world-weary (**156, 157**). If it was shared by many of the upper echelons of the English laity, it would be easy to see that exclusive concern with the fate of the individual soul did indeed facilitate the progress of the English Reformation.

The piety of the Lady Margaret Beaufort, however, fostered by the same intellectual and cultural tradition, involved no renunciation of her wider responsibilities to her tenants or in the government of the realm (**181**). Thomas More, whose faith was more sophisticated than that of any country gentleman, publicly defended the popular manifestations of orthodox religion (**66**). The vast majority of squires and merchants continued to the end to pour their resources into churches which served the wider community. If some perceived that their own religious lives had an added, or different, dimension, most were not constrained in their apparently enthusiastic leadership of communal religious effort. The great strength of the medieval Catholic church was that it could provide satisfaction and solace at a multitude of different levels. This it continued to do, for all but a tiny minority, until fundamental religious changes were enforced by political action. Only then, perhaps, did the experience of private religion, divorced from ceremony and ritual, make it easier for the social elite than for the generality of the population to accept the abolition of the outward forms of the medieval faith.

Part Three: Assessment

8 The Popularity and Diversity of Late Medieval Religion

It is constructive to consider the last century of the pre-Reformation church in England in the wider context of ecclesiastical history, and most particularly in the light of the 'propensity of medieval religious culture to turn repeatedly on itself in critique and reform' (**182**, p. 552). The similarities between the impassioned pleas for the amendment of life uttered by orthodox reformers in the twelfth century and those delivered from early sixteenth-century pulpits are more remarkable than any slight shifts in emphasis; yet historians have tended to interpret the vigorous castigation of abuses in the earlier period as a sign of vitality within an institution intent on its own reform, but to see late medieval complaints as a despairing lamentation over irreversible decline and decay. Many of the abuses within the clerical order which had scandalised twelfth-century reformers had, in fact, been eliminated or at least radically curtailed by the year 1500, and acceptance of the Christian code was far more widespread amongst the laity. The very records from which catalogues of late medieval clerical and monastic misdemeanours can be compiled are themselves testimony to the institutional implementation of reforming ideals and of official determination to root out and punish violators of the demanding code which governed the life of the clergy.

Despite the reiteration of ancient complaints, to the historian who seeks to measure performance by human standards and who is able to draw comparisons with earlier and later periods, the institutions of the English church in the early sixteenth century do not appear to have been in urgent need of radical reform. After a brief hiatus during the reign of Henry VI, when theory was compromised by the feeble practical performance of that pious king, the crown had re-established its leadership in ecclesiastical affairs, most significantly in the matter of appointments. The bishops selected by the Yorkist and early Tudor kings constituted a worthy body of men who endeavoured conscientiously to discharge the multitude of tasks imposed upon them by long tradition, and who for the most part did not abandon their religious responsibilities even when burdened by the foremost offices of state. Among the remainder of the higher clergy, salaried by the revenues of archdeaconries and cathedral prebends, there were few negligent pluralists who fulfilled no useful function within society. The vast majority of the resident parish clergy, both beneficed incumbents and stipendiary chaplains, despite increasing economic hardship, attempted to serve God and their flocks according to the demands of the canon law and the sound advice of pastoral manuals; and although they undoubtedly fell far short of the educational standards demanded by humanist scholars, they apparently did their work to the satisfaction of the vast majority of their parishioners. If the religious orders in general were no longer the spiritual force that they had been in those times when the Benedictines, Cistercians, and friars had in turn provided the yardstick by which the church at large was measured, the Carthusians and Bridgettines nevertheless now took the lead in the dissemination of modes of piety grounded in the monastic experience, yet relevant beyond the cloister. There was little manifestation of lay hostility to monasticism, and there were few problems which could not have been solved by a judicious amalgamation of houses.

There were structural weaknesses within the English church, the most obvious of which was the tendency towards particularism. The maintenance of the ancient rights and privileges of individual offices and corporations too often took priority over the wider interests of the English church as a whole. Internal conflicts which had raged for centuries continued unresolved and burst out anew, and loyalty to a particular local church or to a religious order might easily obscure the greater good, even in the minds of diligent and committed churchmen. The hostility which had originated in the thirteenth century between the friars on the one hand and the bishops and parochial clergy on the other was still a live issue (1). Several religious orders, and some great Benedictine houses, struggled to maintain the exemption from external control other than that of the Papacy which had been granted to them centuries before, in an age when the church was not organised on a national basis (56, 78, 152). The diocesan bishops vociferously resisted the alleged erosion of their rights and revenues by archbishops of Canterbury or papal legates (71, 138). The English church was no more divided at the end of the Middle Ages than it had been in the thirteenth century, but these divisions were perhaps more obvious because they stood in the way of the determined and realistic efforts of Cardinals Morton and Wolsey to create order and uniformity within a national church. Internal dissension within the clerical order provided ammunition for those small but influential groups which for various reasons had a vested interest in the limitation of ecclesiastical authority, most particularly the practitioners of the common law and the political opponents of Wolsey. Most of the great debates within the English church were conducted on a public stage in London – the Carmelite attack on the secular clergy in the 1460s, the probate dispute between Canterbury and its suffragans argued out in Convocation or even in the streets of the capital, and the great debate on benefit of clergy in 1515. Such spectacles may have been a factor in the creation of that dissatisfaction with ecclesiastical institutions expressed by some literate Londoners, which does not seem to have affected the country as a whole. Internecine disputes within the church also made it infinitely more difficult to present a united front when the moment of crisis came, and it may be that the greatest indictment of Wolsey as papal legate is that, in attempting to achieve his ends by aggression rather than by accommodation, he exacerbated divisions within the leadership of the church rather than cemented the solidarity of a fine bench of bishops. In this, if in little else, there is a marked similarity between him and Thomas Becket three and a half centuries before.

These divisions, however, were a matter of ecclesiastical politics and did not adversely affect the church's discharge of its pastoral role or the faith of the English people. The volume of complaint against those who exercised the parochial ministry from the laity who have, according to conventional wisdom, been regarded as anticlerical, and who were presented at visitations with a forum for the airing of grievances, is remarkably small. It was, admittedly, no consolation for the inhabitants of those few parishes which were neglected that the vast majority of English communities were satisfied with their priest, but there is much evidence that complaints were heard and acted upon, and the listing by the historian of entertaining or distressing scandals without reference to normality projects a grossly distorted picture. The most bitter denunciation was of priests who through negligence or malice denied to their flock the spiritual benefits and the solace of the sacraments of the church. The general confidence in the efficacy of these, and most particularly of the Eucharist, is revealed by the endowment by all social classes, according to their means, of multitudinous masses, and by popular enthusiasm for enrolment in confraternities, whose primary function was to secure the salvation of their members by devotions which were utterly orthodox.

Late medieval religion has often been seen as oppressive, characterised by this desperate search for salvation through masses and by the tyranny of confession and penance – the priesthood had a stranglehold over the laity by their monopolisation of the sacraments indispensable for the attainment of eternal life [**doc. 8**]. The majority of confessors, however, did little more than enforce social norms in an annual ritual, and there were frequent complaints that friars gave easy absolution which undermined the authority of the parish priest. Probably only a small minority of people experienced the deep feelings of guilt which came from the frequent examination of conscience advocated by spiritual writers, and of these a large proportion would choose, if not actually employ, their own private confessor (**121**). It was the laypeople themselves, rather than a profiteering priestly caste, who insisted upon the multiplication of masses, and in the early fifteenth century the church in England was hard-pressed to fulfil the demand. It is understandable that in an age of endemic plague there should be a widespread terror of sudden death which might take the victim spiritually unprepared, yet the contrast between the eras before and after the onslaught of the Black Death has perhaps been over-emphasised. The lavish endowment by Henry VII of masses for his soul has been taken as an example of late medieval spiritual neurosis, but it is probable that he expended no greater proportion of his revenues on the quest for salvation than had, for example, William the Conqueror in his three great monastic foundations and other benefactions. Great men in any age have of necessity done much for which they need to atone. The financing by the fifteenth-century aristocracy of masses to be celebrated in perpetuity for their souls and the participation of the lower ranks of society in the same process through their membership of confraternities is paralleled in an earlier age by the establishment by the Anglo-Norman magnates of a plethora of religious houses and by the multitude of grants to the monks by the free peasantry of half-acres or rents of a few pennies. One of the constant strands of medieval popular religion was the belief that salvation was available to mankind, but that the individual had to work to attain eternal beatitude. The shift of endowments from the monasteries to chantry foundations, ranging from colleges established by the great to the service of a single priest at a side-altar of a parish church, is a symptom of increasing lay initiative. The founder could exercise far greater control over the liturgical forms and charitable and educational functions of a chantry than he could have done by passive participation in the spiritual benefits of a great monastic house regulated by the traditions of its own order.

The ecclesiastical authorities themselves encouraged greater lay participation in the formulation of religious practice, and it has been suggested that, following the great campaign of spiritual instruction inaugurated by the Fourth Lateran Council of 1215, Christianity in western Europe in the early fourteenth century became, for the first time since its earliest days, a popular religion (**182**). It was the ever-increasing numbers of literate laypeople who responded most eagerly to the church's invitation. They remained a small minority, but they were an influential one, for although literacy did filter remarkably low down the social scale, a high proportion of those able to read the many devotional texts offered to them came from the ranks of the aristocracy, gentry and merchant oligarchy. Many of the more devout amongst them attempted to live more 'religiously', adapting the monastic regime to the milieu of their own households. Only a few pious widows would make a vow of celibacy, but there are many indications of increasing insistence on strict sexual morality. Such people bridged the gulf between the 'two Christianities' of the earlier Middle Ages, and their experience of religion was perhaps closer to that of the priestly order than to that of their illiterate lay neighbours. It has been suggested that this new religious environment was the seedbed of the English Reformation, that literacy combined with the privacy allowed by elevated social status led to contempt for the faith of the people, characterised by superstition and ritual and increasingly regarded as vulgar (**40**). This coincides with the observation, in the wider context of western Europe in the age of the Renaissance, that there was a shift from the ideal of Christian brotherhood to that of Christian fatherhood, exercised within the pious family unit (a humanist ideal, but prefigured in practice in late medieval England) (**101**). These are most valuable insights into the nature of the religious transformation of the sixteenth century, but some caution is necessary. Until the implementation by the state of the various doctrinal changes which followed the breach with Rome, Englishmen and women who practised the new modes of piety within their own households also belonged to confraternities and took the lead in communal building projects; they were instrumental in the growing popularity and official recognition of new cults associated with Jesus and His Mother; and their devotions continued to centre on the Mass, celebrated only by ordained members of the priesthood. It is almost certain that such people experienced their deepest religious emotions in private, but this interiorisation occurred within a framework of belief which was entirely orthodox. The great strength of the late medieval church was that it could accommodate a wide diversity of practices which brought satisfaction to people of many different levels of intellect and social status.

In the early sixteenth century the church in England, long organised as a national unit but subject to Rome in matters of faith and recognising papal jurisdiction in a wide range of issues acknowledged as spiritual, appeared to be extremely secure. The major crisis had occurred one hundred and fifty years before, when the Great Schism had inaugurated a prolonged debate on the nature of Christian authority; when the Lollard heresy had gained widespread support at Oxford University and the royal court, and its adherents had proposed an alternative form of ecclesiastical government; when there had been many manifestations of resentment against churchmen as landlords attempting in the wake of the Black Death to enforce the performance of services by their tenantry; and when there had been a dramatic drop in clerical recruitment. It is the task of the historian of Tudor religion to explain how the Reformation happened in sixteenth-century England. The medievalist must turn his attention to a question just as urgent: why did it *not* occur in the far more propitious circumstances of the late fourteenth century?

Part Four: Documents

An Italian view of English religion

This extract is taken from the observations of an Italian visitor to England, and was probably the report on the country sent to the Venetian Senate by Andrea Trevisano, head of a mission despatched to King Henry VII in 1497.

Although they all attend Mass every day and say many Paternosters in public (the women carrying long rosaries in their hands, and any who can read taking the office of Our Lady with them, and with some companion reciting it in the church verse by verse in a low voice, after the manner of churchmen), they always hear Mass on Sunday in their parish church and give liberal alms, because they may not offer less than a piece of money, of which fourteen are equivalent to a golden ducat; nor do they omit any form incumbent upon good Christians; there are, however, many who have various opinions concerning religion . . .

But above all are their riches displayed in the church treasures; for there is not a parish church in the kingdom so mean as not to possess crucifixes, candlesticks, censers, patens and cups of silver, besides many other ornaments worthy of a cathedral church in the same metal.

Sneyd (**25**), pp. 23, 29; reprinted (**27**), pp. 195, 198.

document 2
Royal control of the English church

(a) *The following extracts from the records of the Convocation of Canterbury of January 1489 illustrate the pressure of the crown on the English church for taxation. The grant of a fixed sum, rather than a tenth of income, was an innovation. In the same year Parliament granted a lay subsidy of £75,000.*

On 19 January there entered the chapter house John Dynham, Treasurer of England, John earl of Oxford, Thomas earl of Derby and others of the king's council, sent by the king. The Treasurer elegantly explained that the king was enormously grateful for the charity and the concern they had shown for his majesty and the honour of his realm, and asked for their perseverance in this, promising to be a willing defender of the rights and liberties of the church in England. He then announced that the king, partly because of the request of the community of the realm expressed in the present Parliament, partly and more especially to counter the threat posed to the realm by the king of France, was anxious to defend the realm, and in this enterprise he needed the succour of the prelates and clergy of the province, not only their prayers but also their financial aid. The archbishop said that he would confer with Convocation, and as it was late adjourned proceedings to the following day . . .

On 27 February, in the archbishop's presence, the prolocutor granted to the king, in the name of all the clergy, a great subsidy of £25,000, to be paid in two instalments, and as two tenths of the province would scarcely amount to the total of the subsidy, he conceded two whole tenths from ecclesiastical benefices and possessions, taxed and untaxed, which by custom paid tenths, with this provision, that when the subsidy of £25,000 had been paid, the prelates and clergy should be acquitted and exonerated from any further payment. He also granted two charitable subsidies to the archbishop, for the praise of God and the defence of the church in England.

Harper-Bill (**14**), pp. 30–2, nos 103, 118.

(**b**)   *Charles Booth was nominated by Henry VIII to the bishopric of Hereford on 22 April 1516, three days after the death of his predecessor. He was given custody of the temporalities during the vacancy of the see on 17 May, was provided by the pope to the see on 21 July, was consecrated on 30 November, and had the temporalities restored to him as bishop on 19 February 1517. The sequence of events, and his oath, reveal the constitutive role of the king in his appointment.*

Homage done and oath of fealty made by the bishop to the king.
   I renounce and utterly forsake all manner of words and

sentences contained in the pope's bull granted to me of the bishopric of Hereford which be or in any wise may be prejudicial or hurtful to your highness, to your crown or dignity royal, and therefore I put me wholly in your grace, beseeching the same to have restitution of the temporalities of my said bishopric which I claim to hold of your grace. And also I shall be faithful and true, and faith and troth I shall bear unto you, sovereign lord Henry, by the grace of God king of England and France and lord of Ireland, and to your heirs, kings of the same, and diligently shall be attendant to your business and counsel after my cunning and power, and your counsel I shall keep secret and truly conceal. And the service due for the temporalities of my said bishopric of Hereford which I claim to hold of your grace I shall truly do, and to you and your commandments as far as to me attains for my said temporalities I shall be obeisant, and if anything I know prejudicial or hurtful to your royal person or estate, I shall resist it to the best of my power, or at the least give thereof knowledge to your highness or to such of your council as shall give your grace knowledge thereof, with all diligence that may goodly be done. So help me God and the holy Gospels.

Bannister (**2**), p. 18 (spelling here modernised).

document 3

Papal dispensations

The following dispensations are taken from the registers of Pope Sixtus IV (1471–84). They record permission granted to individuals, at their request, to deviate in some way from the provisions of the canon law which were incumbent on all Christians.

(**a**) *Dispensation to hold two benefices with cure of souls.*
27 October 1474. Pius II dispensed John Manyngham, perpetual vicar of St Margaret's Lowestoft, in the diocese of Norwich, M.A., to hold for life with the said vicarage any benefice, or without the vicarage any two other benefices, with cure or otherwise incompatible, and to resign or exchange them, the said dispensation stating that the value of the said vicarage does not exceed twenty-six marks sterling, and that John was of noble birth.
At his recent petition, containing that if the salary of a chaplain

to serve the said church and other burdens etc. be deducted the said value does not exceed twenty-six marks sterling, but that it is greater if they be not deducted, and although John's mother was of noble birth his father was not, the pope hereby (seeing that John would have obtained the said dispensation from the said pope with equal ease notwithstanding the said statements, especially because he is an Englishman and because the said pope and preceding popes have been more liberal in granting such dispensations to Englishmen than to those of other nations) validates the said dispensation from the date thereof.

(b) *Commutation of a pilgrimage for a money payment.*
29 September 1481. To Richard Lessi, clerk of the diocese of York. Commutation, at the petition also of Edward king of England, of his vows to visit the shrines of the apostles at Rome and also in the Holy Land, and the Lord's Sepulchre, into a sum of one hundred gold ducats of the *Camera*, which he has paid to the pope's datary in aid of the crusade and in aid of the fleet which, with a great number of triremes, the pope has prepared against the Turks; with dispensation and absolution from the said vows.

(c) *Dispensation for marriage within the prohibited degrees.*
1482. Absolution of John Sothel, layman, and Alice Waslyn, married woman, of the diocese of York, from excommunication incurred by marrying, not in ignorance that they were related in the second and second degrees of kindred, because although they were not descended from the same grandfather, they were descended from the same grandmother. The pope dispenses them to contract marriage anew, and decrees present and future offspring thereof legitimate.

(d) *Dispensation from the obligations of fasting.*
14 June 1479. To Thomas de Montegumbri, knight, of the diocese of London. Indult for him, who is wont to be ill after fasting, at the petition of John Doget, treasurer of Chichester, to eat, with two companions, flesh and milk-meats in Lent (except in Holy Week), and on other days on which fasting is enjoined and the eating of flesh forbidden, and not to be bound to fast on the said days.

Calendar of Entries in the Papal Registers, (**7**), pp. 38–9, 102, 110, 249.

Papal indulgences

(a) *The upper chapel of St Stephen's, Westminster, rebuilt in the 1460s, housed a closet which contained an image of the Virgin encrusted in jewels, and known as St Mary of the Pew. This document is an example of a partial indulgence, and illustrates the belief in the efficacy of masses in hastening the passage to Heaven of the souls of the departed.*

27 April 1476. Statute and decree in perpetuity that all faithful of both sexes who, being penitent and confessed, visit on the Ascension of Our Lord, the feast of St Stephen the Protomartyr and on the commemoration of All Souls, from the first to the second vespers of the said Ascension and feasts, the chapel of St Mary the Virgin, vulgarly called the chapel of the Pew in the collegiate church of St Stephen the Protomartyr within the king's palace of Westminster in the diocese of London (to which Anthony Woodville, earl Rivers, brother of Elizabeth queen of England, and other faithful of those parts have a singular devotion) and give alms for its maintenance etc., shall gain an indulgence of fifteen years and as many quarantines for each of the said three days, and that the souls for whom masses are celebrated in the said chapel shall gain the indulgence which is gained by the souls of the departed for whom masses are celebrated in the chapel of St Mary *de Scala Dei* in the church, or without the church, of the Cistercian monastery of St Anastasius without the walls of Rome. If similar indulgence, not yet expired, have been granted by the present pope, the present letters. shall be null and void.

Calendar of Entries in the Papal Registers, (**7**), p. 498.

(b) *The Italian Polydore Vergil came to England in 1502 as deputy papal collector, and remained until 1553, almost half a century after losing that office. The first version of his* Anglica Historia, *originally commissioned by Henry VII, was completed in 1531. The Jubilee indulgence was first granted in 1300, and by the late fifteenth century was offered every twenty-five years.*

This was the year 1500 from the birth of our Saviour. In the very same year the Jubilee was celebrated at Rome, in which a plenary remission of all sins was offered to those who visited the threshold of the apostles. And since far-off peoples could not easily or without loss to themselves reach the city of Rome because of the wars which were raging in Italy at the time, lest on this account good Christians should be deprived of the benefit of heavenly grace, Pope Alexander VI therefore sent several legates in various directions to proclaim the Jubilee to those people situated at long distances from Italy. Gaspar Ponce was sent to England, a Spaniard by birth and distinguished by both scholarship and virtuous character; armed with papal authority, he ordered the festival to be observed in all areas owing allegiance to the English king. He conferred on Englishmen the benefit of divine grace, by which all stain of sin was obliterated, and he received from them great sums of money, through which the pope was to have been better able to turn his attention to the holy war against the Turks; this war the pope had proclaimed that he would soon undertake, but it has not, however, yet been embarked upon. For alas, evil spirits so pervert our minds that, ignoring the real enemies of our religion, we allow them to enjoy prolonged tranquillity, while we turn our armed and bloody hands against ourselves and our own limbs.

Hay (**15**), pp. 119–21.

document 5

The state of monasticism

The provincial chapter of the Benedictine Order states its objections to Cardinal Wolsey's proposed reforms (12 November 1519 or February 1520). The same resistance to change had been expressed a century before in response to King Henry V's articles.

Most reverend father in Christ and right respected lord, we have with due reverence read from beginning to end the schedule of statutes for the reform of the Order of St Benedict sent to us last week by your reverend lordship, and although we have found therein many proposals which should be embraced by good monks with all diligence and a joyful spirit, there are nevertheless included such regulations as seem to us to savour of greater austerity than can possibly, in these unhappy times of ours, be observed by monks. Of these there is in England, without argument, a very large number, and so great and so large are their communities and convents that it would be extraordinarily difficult, at least by human agency, suddenly to reimpose this austerity on such a multitude without the outbreak of murmuring and the incitement of a great spirit of rebellion. We therefore, the humble and unworthy ministers of the same Order, devoted servants and obedient sons of your most sacred paternity, prostrate at your feet in prayer, humbly beg and implore that your most gracious lordship should mercifully cast your eyes upon us and the foresaid Order, so that by your holy and sagacious industry, by your divine intellect so much greater than that of other men, in short by your superabundant wisdom, all that pertains to this future reform of monks may be modified and those things which are hard and difficult may be accomplished in such a way that the feeble monks of our religion may not be driven to flight and apostasy nor by the prompting of the devil (which God forbid) rise up against their pastors, neither may those who have determined to enter our Order shrink away from their intention or abandon it because of excessive rigour and austerity; for it is beyond the shadow of a doubt that if the reform of the foresaid Order were to tend in all things towards the greatest austerity and strictness, we should not have monks, at least not in respectable numbers sufficient to populate so many and such great monasteries. If, indeed, there were in England as many communities of the Carthusians or of the Orders of St Bridget and of the Friars Minor of the Observance as there are of Benedictine monks, we just cannot see from where they would recruit such a multitude as would enable them to be maintained. In our age, when the world is now declining towards its end, there are extremely few men, indeed they are most rare, who desire an ascetic life and observance of the Rule. Whatever we say in these matters, holy father, we do so not because we can suggest anything at all that can be done which has not already been amply considered and reviewed by your holy lordship, but rather because, roused in our emotions, we have clearly revealed how greatly in these matters we need the consolation and aid of your most reverend lordship, to whom, most reverend father and respected lord, we commend ourselves all in our want, with all humility, obedience and reverence that we may show to so holy a father, and with our constant allegiance and supplication.

Most faithful intercessors for your salvation, your humble servants and most unworthy ministers of the Order of Black Monks in England, now gathered by your command at London.

Pantin (**24**), vol iii, pp. 123–4 (here translated from Latin).

document 6
Some cases from an archdeacon's court book

This session of the court of the Archdeacon of Buckingham was conducted by the deputy of the archdeacon's Official at Aylesbury, where the church was annexed to a prebend of Lincoln Cathedral. Despite some welcome colourful detail, these cases are typical of the business which came before such courts. The exemplary penance imposed on a practitioner of magical arts is noteworthy.

Proceedings before Master John London, commissary and Official, on 5 March 1520 in the parish church of Aylesbury.

John Gorhill, stipendiary priest in the prebendal church, exhibited his letters of ordination.

Laurence Tailour, one of the churchwardens of the parish of Leckhampstead, appeared and stated that he was prepared to swear on the Gospels that the churchyard of Leckhampstead had been properly set in order by All Saints day last, as had been ordered by the Official during the last archidiaconal visitation, but John Hawkyns, the other churchwarden, stated that this was not so. Because of his manifest presumption in offering to perjure himself, the judge enjoined on Laurence Tailour the following public penance, that he should on each Sunday during Lent process barefoot before the cross around the parish church, and in penitential fashion he should each Sunday offer to the priest at high mass a wax candle, and at the next court session he should appear before the judge to demonstrate that he had performed this penance. Afterwards the judge, at the request of many venerable persons, adjourned this penance until the coming of Dr Cocks [the Official].

Aylesbury prebendal church. There appeared William Adderbury and Thomas Davy of Walton, accused by a certain Robert Walton of incontinence with Alice Frawnces. The judge accepted their request that they should be granted a term to purge themselves, each separately, at the next court session, and instructed them to purge themselves each with five honest neighbours, and also admonished Robert to purge himself on the same day with six oath-helpers. And Robert Walton promised that in the next court he would produce two trustworthy witnesses to prove that Thomas Davy lay suspiciously on Alice's stomach, and lay with her in a meadow called 'the milmede' for the time that it took William Simon to prepare an acre of meadow for the plough.

There appeared Henry Lyllingstone of Broughton, accused that he commonly uses magical arts to cure various persons. He admitted his reputation and the charge, in that when men came to him he did use such a remedy, saying in English: 'Jhesus that savid bothe you and me from all maner deseasses, I ask for seynt cherite Our Lord iff it be your wille'; and he said that this remedy was generally beneficial to all sick people. He also had another cure which he said was especially effective for those suffering from stones or colic, which was horsehound, Alexander's Foot and the red heads of marigolds, mixed and pounded and cooked with good beer and treacle, and then given to sick people to drink, and he said that this medicine had cured many people. Asked whether he was literate and where he had learned of these cures, he said he was not literate, but had always had this knowledge by the grace of God. The judge ordered Henry to swear upon the Gospels that he would never in the future use such remedies or any similar, and imposed the following public penance, that every Sunday in Lent, barefoot and clad only in a smock, he should go before the cross in the parochial procession at Broughton, holding in his right hand a wax candle which he should offer to the priest at the offertory during high mass; and that every Wednesday and Friday for a year he should fast on bread and water; and that next Michaelmas he should make a barefoot pilgrimage to the shrine of St Mary of Walsingham. Henry Lillingstone professed himself willing to perform all the foresaid penances and swore the oath.

A citation was issued against Richard Balle of Amersham, at the instance of Oliver Bakthorn and Thomas Tailour of Ellesborough, in that the foresaid Balle had impregnated a woman whose name he did not know and had fathered by her a little boy now in the custody of Thomas Tailour, and Balle was unwilling to give anything for the maintenance of the child, as he was bound to do.

William Hedderseth of Haddenham *versus* William Barnard of the same, in a case of defamation. The parties appeared. Hedderseth alleged that last January in the workshop of Thomas Johnson, smith, in Haddenham, Barnard had uttered the following scandalous words, that he had seen Hedderseth to lie with and have carnal intercourse with a certain Joan Robyns of Haddenham in an enclosure called 'Fisher's Close', or other scandalous words to the same effect, whereby Hedderseth stood defamed in the eyes of good and weighty persons. Wherefore he asked that Barnard should be punished according to the sanctions of canon law, and that expenses which he had incurred and would incur should be awarded against Barnard. Barnard denied the accusation and intended to contest the case. The judge instructed Hedderseth to produce witnesses for the first time at the next court session and to purge himself with five honest neighbours, and he ordered Barnard to be present.

On the same day there were proceedings in another defamation case, three matrimonial suits, and a case concerning the tithe of lambs and wool. Six persons who had failed to appear before the court were pronounced contumacious and suspended from church, and probate of a last testament was granted.

Elvey (**10**), pp. 256–8, no 349 (here translated from Latin).

document 7

The sacraments of the church

These extracts from the statutes of Archbishop John Pecham (1279–92) were incorporated by William Lyndwood (d. 1446) into his definitive collection of the legislation of the province of Canterbury. They emphasise the centrality to the faith of the sacraments, and most especially of the Eucharist.

(**a**) There are seven sacraments of grace, of which the dispensers are the prelates of the church, and of which five should be received by all Christians, that is baptism, confirmation, penance and the Eucharist, at due times, and extreme unction, which should only be administered to those who appear, because of signs of grave infirmity, to be approaching close to the peril of death. To such, if it is possible, it should be given while they are of sound mind, but if it happens that they are frenzied or suffering any mental aberration, we consider that nevertheless this sacrament should be administered to them with confidence, for we believe and have learned by experience that to a person however frenzied, if he is a child of predestination, the reception of the sacrament will bring benefit, either that he may experience an interval of lucidity or at least that he will obtain spiritual benefit by the increase of grace. There are two other sacraments, orders and matrimony, of which the first is suitable for those who are perfect, but the second, from the time of the New Testament, is only suitable for those imperfect, but we believe that grace is bestowed by the strength of the sacrament, if it is contracted with sincerity.

Lyndwood, (**20**), book 1, title 7, chapter 4 (here translated from Latin).

(**b**) Priests should take care that when they give holy communion to simple people, at Easter or at any other time, they should instruct them carefully that in the form of the bread is given to them the Body and Blood of our Lord, indeed the whole Christ, living and true, who is whole in the form of the sacrament.

They should teach them also that what is at the same time drunk from the chalice is not a sacrament, but pure wine given to them to drink so that they may more easily swallow the sacrament which they have taken. For in minor churches it is permitted only to the celebrant to take the Blood in the form of consecrated wine. They should instruct them also that, having taken the sacrament in their mouth, they should not break it up with their teeth, but should swallow it down as little broken as possible, lest any small part of it remain between their teeth or elsewhere.

Lyndwood (**20**), book 1, title 1, chapter 2 (here translated from Latin).

document 8

Confession and penance

This canon, derived by Lyndwood from a fourteenth-century diocesan statute, illustrates the skills encouraged in the confessor by pastoral manuals, and also the social functions of confession and penance.

The priest, in enjoining penance, should diligently note the circumstances of guilt, the quality of the person, the kind of sin, the time, place and cause, how long was the continuance in sin, and the devotion of spirit shown by the penitent. Having considered these things and diligently and discreetly pondered them, he should enjoin upon the penitent greater or lesser penance. Also the priest should choose a common place to hear confessions, where he may be seen generally by all those in the church, and the priest shall not hear in secret places the confession of anyone, and especially of women, except in case of urgent necessity or because of the infirmity of the penitent. Also no priest shall accept another's parishioner for penance except by the permission of his priest or of the bishop. Also the priest should enjoin upon a wife such penance that she be not suspected by her husband of any secret and great sin, and the same should be observed for a husband. Also for theft, rapine, fraud, and especially for the withholding of tithes or the subtraction of any ecclesiastical right, priests should take care that they enjoin only penance which includes satisfaction and restitution to be made to those who have suffered injury or damage, since the sin is not discharged unless that which has been removed is restored. Also in crimes which are, very great or heinous, or when he is in doubt, the priest should consult the bishop or him to whom is delegated his authority, or wise and discreet persons, assured by whose advice he may know whom and in what way he may bind and loose. And lest, God forbid, the penitent should fall into desperation, the priest should diligently admonish him to do in the meantime any good that he may, that God may lighten his heart unto penitence. And this too shall he do also to him who confesses his sin but will not abstain from it, in which case the gift of absolution cannot be given, since it is ordained that pardon may be given only to him who sets himself aright. Also priests should take care that they do not enquire the names or the sins of those with whom the penitent has sinned, but only the circumstances and the nature of the sin, for it is written: 'God, I have shewed to Thee mine own life and not any other's', and the confession must be his own, not another's.

Lyndwood (**20**), book 5, title 16, chapter 7 (here translated from Latin).

document 9
A religious confraternity

This is a synopsis of the certificate returned to the Royal Chancery in 1389 by the Guild of Corpus Christi in the church of St Michael-on-the-Hill, Lincoln, founded in 1350. In its emphasis on religious observance, and specifically on the veneration of the Eucharist, and its incidental social benefits for distressed members, it is typical of a multitude of English confraternities established in the late Middle Ages.

Founded in honour of our Lord Jesus Christ and of His precious Body and Blood, and of the most holy Sepulchre of that most glorious Body, and of the Virgin Mother Mary, and of all the saints of God. Thirteen square candles to be set round the

Sepulchre on the day of the Preparation, and from that day to the octave they burn on festival days at high mass; three round candles to burn continuously from the day of the Preparation to the Resurrection. A great torch to be provided for the Corpus Christi procession. Before the procession all are to assemble and receive garlands of one pattern, and so make procession to the cathedral, where each offers a farthing at the high altar. The great torch is borne before the Body of Christ when being carried to the sick, also it burns at the elevation on six principal days. Four soul-candles, with others, burn round the hearse of a brother. At the funeral mass the grace-man and warden each offer one penny from the guild fund and each brother offers as he will, and gives one half-penny for bread in soul-alms. The guild banner is borne to the house of a dead brother and there displayed publicly in order to show that the deceased was a member of the guild. Thence, with the great light, it precedes the corpse to the church. They will have a guild priest to sing for souls when God shall have multiplied their resources. Mass to be celebrated for living and dead brothers on the octave of Corpus Christi, the bell tolling on its vigil.

Burial, if need be, is to be at the guild's expense. A penny a day shall be given to brethren in cases of accidental poverty.

If a member goes on pilgrimage to Jerusalem, each brother gives him one penny. If he goes to St James [Compostella] or St Peter and St Paul [Rome], all the brethren lead him or her to the cross before the hospital of the Innocents outside Lincoln, and when he returns meet him there and bring him to the mother church.

Westlake (**92**), pp. 167–8.

document 10
Last testament of Richard Berne, citizen and mercer of London

This testament was written on 13 November 1525, and probate was granted on 29 November 1525. The document here summarised provides an excellent illustration of a wide variety of pious and charitable works, the discharge of which was considered beneficial to the soul.

Body to be buried in the place near the chapel that he caused to be made in the south aisle of St Magnus church, where he has caused a stone to be laid and where the body of Margaret his late wife lies buried. To the high altar of the same church for tithes forgotten 3s 4d. To the works of the body of the church aforesaid for his burial there 13s 4d. Body to be buried at discretion of executors without any pride or pomp of the world. His debts to be paid. Executors to cause a trental of masses to be said in the church of St Magnus for his soul, his wife's soul and all Christian souls every month once on the Friday for one year after his death; £6 to be disposed among the priests saying the trental for their salary. To the churchwardens of St Magnus 12s to buy bread, wine and wax for the trentals. Every Friday for a year after his death 3s 4d to be disposed by executors or their assigns in bread among poor prisoners as follows: 3s 4d among those in Newgate and another Friday 3s 4d among those of the King's Bench and the next Friday 3s 4d among those in Ludgate and another Friday 3s 4d among those of the Marshalsea and so to continue weekly upon the Friday among the poor prisoners of the said four prison houses.

Executors to provide 200 ells of the best 'vetery canvas' and make thereof shirts and smocks for the poor people in the towns of Bromham, Stagsden and Cranfield in Bedfordshire. To twenty poor householders of Bedford twenty pairs of shop sheets of the best, one pair of sheets to every householder. 40s to be disposed among forty poor householders of the parish of St Magnus, that is 12d each, desiring them to be at his *dirige* and on the morrow at the Mass and offer every of them ¼d. To the fraternity of Papey 13s 4d, desiring them to bear his body to the church and to his grave. 20s to be disposed in meat and drink within a year after his decease to the sick and bed-ridden people in St Bartholomew's hospital in West Smithfield; another 20s to those in St Mary Spitle without Bishopsgate and another 20s among those of St Thomas Spitle in Southwark, Surrey. To the four lazar houses about London 26s 8d, that is 6s 8d each.

To Dorothy Berne daughter of his brother, £10 sterling. To the wife of Brian Morehous of Evesham £6 13s 4d sterling. To Richard Butler, servant of Henry Parker, £3 6s 8d and a black gown. To Nicholas Butler £3 6s 8d and a black gown. To Henry Parker and Agnes his wife a black gown each. To cousin Alice Iseland £10 sterling at full age or marriage. To the fraternity of the Clerks of this noble city 6s 8d. Executors to buy against his burial twelve tapers of wax of 2lb each, and twelve children in surplices bear the said tapers, and to every child 4d for their labour. The twelve torches that shall be left at his burial as follows: two to the high altar of St Magnus church, two to the church of the town of

Bedford, two to Bromham church and two to Stagsden church; two to the brotherhood of the church of St Magnus and the other two to the alms of the said church of St Magnus, the same torches to be occupied there to the honour of God as long as they shall endure.

To each servant in his service at his death, one black gown of the price of 5s a yard. To Richard Berne, son of his brother, £13 6s 8d. To Robert Berne, son of his brother, £13 6s 8d. To Richard Hill, his servant, £13 6s 8d. To John Maynard, his servant, £13 6s 8d. To every woman servant in his house on the day of his death 40s. To Dowse Mudworth, servant of Alexander Plymley mercer, 20s. To Richard Hill, son of Richard Hill cutler, his godson, 20s. To Richard Thornton, his godson, 20s. To Thomas Davyson, the son of John Davyson, to be delivered at lawful age of twenty-one years, £10 sterling, which £10 is to remain in the hands of the masters of the fraternity of Our Blessed Lady and St Thomas the Martyr within the said church of St Magnus, charging them and their successors to find the said Thomas at meat, drink, cloth linen, woollen and bed until he attains twenty-one, and also that the said Thomas have sufficient learning, and if Thomas dies before twenty-one years the £10 is to be delivered to the testator's cousin Alice Iselond if then married or of lawful age, and if she is dead the same £10 to remain to the said fraternity. He forgives John Davyson all debts owing by him to testator at the date of making his will.

To the said fraternity of Our Blessed Lady and St Thomas the Martyr £220 sterling to the following uses: the masters and keepers of the same and their successors shall yearly from Michaelmas 1525 for twenty years provide an honest priest to sing and say Mass within the said church for souls of testator, his wives Margaret and Maryon, his father and mother, his friends and all Christians, and the same priest to be resident at all divine service said and sung in the said church at feast days and holy (*inferial*) days, and he is to be paid £8 per annum for his salary, and at four times a year during the said term he is to say and sing mass of *Scala Celi*, that is to say at Westminster, Savoy or Crossed Friars for the said souls, and he is to have 12d for every mass of *Scala Celi* over and above his yearly salary of £8 sterling. Masters of said fraternity and their successors to keep his obit and anniversary within the said church of St Magnus for souls abovesaid, with *placebo* and *dirige* over the night and mass of requiem on the morrow solemnly by note, with ringing of bells and other obsequies to such an obit accustomed, and said masters are to pay yearly

111

during the said twenty years at the said obit 20s sterling as follows: to the parson or his deputy being at the obit 12d, and to the parish priest for rehearsing names of testator and names aforesaid in the bederoll 12d, and to the masters or keepers of the fraternity being at the obit 3s 4d, that is 20d each, and to the other priests, clerks and conducts of the said church being also at the said obit 4d each, and the residue of the 20s to be spent in bread and drink for the priests, clerks and parishioners of the same parish and in alms for the poor parishioners there and for wax and other charges, by discretion of the said masters. The masters or keepers of said fraternity and their successors are to be bound by a 'sufficient writing obligatory' of the sum of £220 sterling to perform said devise. Within three months of his death his executors are to pay churchwardens of the said church of St Magnus £100 sterling which he bequeathes towards the making of an altar table for the high altar of the said church to be made and 'korved' of the best fashion that may be devised. Executors to pay the churchwardens of the same church for the charge of the 'celyng and karving' over the Crucifix in the rood loft, which John Rypley joiner is bound to make, in part payment whereof the said John has received beforehand £6 13s 4d, and over that to pay all charges of gilding the same works, which testator wills to be gilded after the best manner that may be.

His wife Maryon to have her part and portion of his goods according to the custom of the City of London, and he bequeathes to her £100 sterling over and above her part.

As to disposition of his lands and tenements in the towns and parishes of Bedford, Cranfield and Bromham in Bedfordshire, those persons who stand seised of the same to the use of testator and his heirs after his death are to stand seised to the use of Maryon his wife during her life, and after her decease to use of Richard Berne, son of his brother, and his heirs forever.

Residue to be disposed by executors by advice of overseers in marrying poor maidens, relieving and setting at large poor prisoners, amending 'high noyous waies', singing masses of *Scala Celi* at Westminster, Savoy or Crossed Friars, and in other good works of mercy and charity for the souls abovesaid. His executors to be his wife Maryon, Alexander Plymley, Richard Berne and Robert Berne children of his brother, and to Alexander, Richard and Robert for their labour £6 13s 4d each; any executors causing strife to be excluded by others and not to benefit from any legacy herein. Overseers to be William Huxley, Oliver Leder gentleman,

Bartholomew Barner, Richard Hill and John Maynard, to whom for their labours £6 13s 4d each and a black gown. He revokes former wills.

McGregor (**21**), pp. 125–7.

A devout household

This description of the religious life of Sir Thomas More refers to several characteristic features of the domestic religion of the prosperous and literate laity of late medieval England – private prayer, a place within the establishment set aside for devotions, and edifying religious discussion.

As Sir Thomas More's custom was daily, if he were at home, besides his private prayers, with his children to say the Seven Psalms, Litany and Suffrages following, so was his guise nightly before he went to bed, with his wife, children and household, to go to his chapel and there upon his knees ordinarily to say certain psalms and collects with them. And because he was desirous for godly purposes sometime to be solitary and sequester himself from worldly company, a good distance from his mansion house builded he a place called the New Building, wherein there was a chapel, a library and a gallery. In which, as his use was upon other days to occupy himself in prayer and study together, so on the Friday there usually continued he from morning to evening, spending his time only in devout prayers and spiritual exercises.

And to provoke his wife and children to the desire of heavenly things, he would sometimes use these words unto them:

'It is now no mastery [i.e. achievement] for you children to go to Heaven, for everybody giveth you good counsel, everybody giveth you good example – you see virtue rewarded and vice punished. So that you are carried up to Heaven even by the chins. But if you live the time that no man will give you good counsel, nor no man will give you good example, when you shall see virtue punished and vice rewarded, if you will then stand fast and firmly stick to God, upon pain of my life, though you be but half good, God will allow you for whole good.'

If his wife or any of his children had·been diseased or troubled, he would say unto them: 'We may not look at our pleasure to go to Heaven in featherbeds. It is not the way, for our Lord himself went thither with great pain and by many tribulations, which was the path wherein He walked thither. For the servant may not look to be in better case than his master.'

Sylvester and Harding (**26**), pp. 210–11.

document 12

The fight against heresy

(**a**) *Walter Hilton, writing at the time when John Wyclif's views were gaining ground outside Oxford, expounds on the arrogance of those who maintain opinions condemned by the universal church.*

How pride in heretics is mortal sin.
A heretic sins mortally through pride, because he takes a delight in clinging to his own opinion, maintaining it to be true although it is contrary to God and Holy Church. He will not retract his opinion, but holds to it as truth, and so makes it his god. But he deceives himself, for God and Holy Church are in such unity and accord that whoever opposes one opposes both. Therefore anyone who says that he loves God, and keeps His commandments, but despises Holy Church and disregards the laws and ordinances made by its supreme head for the direction of all Christians, is a liar. He does not choose God, but chooses the love of himself, which is the opposite to the love of God, and in so doing he commits mortal sin. And in the very matter in which he thinks to please God most, he displeases Him most, for he is blind and will not see. Of this blindness and false confidence in one's own opinions the wise man says: There is a way which seems right to a man, but which leads him at length to eternal death (Proverbs xiv, 12). This is especially true of heresy, for other worldly sinners who commit mortal sin and continue in it usually come to recognise their errors and are smitten in conscience that they are not in the right way. But the heretic always supposes that his doings and opinions are good, and that no one is better than he. So he thinks that his own way is right, and therefore feels no qualms of conscience or humility of heart. Indeed, unless God in His mercy sends him humility while he lives, he will in the end go to Hell.

Yet he thinks that he has done well, and that he will win the joys of Heaven by his teachings.

Hilton (**17**), book 1, chapter 58, pp. 70–1.

(b) *This abjuration by a Herefordshire Lollard encapsulates most of the main tenets of later Lollardy.*

Abjuration of John Croft, made in the chapter house of Hereford cathedral in February 1505.

In the name of God, Amen. I, John Crofte, of the parish of Eardisley within the diocese of Hereford, willingly acknowledge before you, masters Owen Pole, John Wardroper and Richard Judde, commissaries of the reverend father in God Richard bishop of Hereford, in this behalf lawfully assigned and deputed, that I have had in my ward and keeping divers books containing heresies and errors against Christian faith and the determination of all holy church, which books I have read and declared oftentimes privily and openly, on holy days and feast days, before many divers persons, reading, declaring and teaching against the blessed sacrament of the altar otherwise than I ought to have done, also against the sacrament of confession to priests and penance for satisfaction of sin, also against the solemnisation of the sacrament of matrimony, calling it exorcisms and deceits (*coninzations*). Also I have read and declared against our holy father the pope, showing that he hath not the power of binding and loosing that Christ gave to Peter, but in usurping that power upon him he maketh himself Antichrist. Also I have read and taught against the veneration and worship of images standing in churches, calling them idols (*maummetis*), and against the enshrining of saints' bones in gold and silver, and the hanging about them of the same. These errors, heresies and false opinions afore rehearsed, damned and reproved by authority of all holy church, in especial, and all other in general, I forswear, abjure and forsake, promising that from henceforth I shall never read, declare or teach, affirm, believe neither hold any errors, heresies or opinions contrary to the determination of all holy church, neither shall I maintain or favour any person or persons suspect or guilty in these premises or any other contrary to the faith and determination of all holy church, or any books of such false errors, but I shall detect and show them unto my lord Bishop of Hereford for the time being, my ordinary, or otherwise to his officers, in as goodly haste as I can or may. And all such penance as shall be by you or any of your commissaries above said to me for my trespass in this behalf enjoined, I shall meekly and devoutly perform and fulfil, so God help me at His holy doom, and these holy Gospels of God. In witness whereof I make this sign of the cross with mine + own hand.

Bannister (**1**), pp. 66–7 (spelling here modernised).

Glossary

Advowson   The right of presentation to an ecclesiastical benefice or living.

Appropriation   Annexation to an ecclesiastical corporation (e.g. cathedral or monastery) of the tithes and endowments intended for the maintenance of a priest in a parish.

Archdeacon   Ecclesiastical officer next in dignity to a bishop, with jurisdictional powers over a division of a diocese.

Archdeaconry   Territorial division of a diocese subject to the jurisdiction of the archdeacon.

Benefice   An ecclesiastical living, e.g. rectory, vicarage.

Cantarist   A priest serving a chantry (see below).

Chantry   An endowment for the maintenance of priests to sing masses, usually for the soul of the founder.

Chapter   The members of a collegiate church (e.g. cathedral) who hold prebends (or portions of the revenues) therein, or the members of a monastic house; the meeting of such a body for discussion.

Church-ale   A social meeting held to raise funds for the parish church.

(in) commendam   Tenure of a benefice, with enjoyment of its revenues, granted either until an incumbent is provided, or for life.

Compurgation   The action of clearing a defendant from a charge by the oaths of a number of others.

Confraternity   A brotherhood; in the present context one formed for religious purposes.

Exempt   Not subject to superior authority, e.g. exempt from episcopal authority and subject only to the pope.

Glossary

Glebe   Portion of land assigned to a parish priest as part of his living.

Indulgence   Remission of the punishment which is still due to sin after sacramental absolution by a priest, this remission being valid in the eyes of God; granted by the pope or (limited to forty days) by a bishop.

Indult   Licence granted by the pope, authorising something which the canon law does not ordinarily allow.

Legate   An ecclesiastic deputed to act for the pope; the archbishop of Canterbury was traditionally *legatus natus* (native legate) but his authority was superseded by a legate *a latere* (commissioned directly by the pope).

Mendicant   A beggar. Hence those orders of friars who, in theory, held no communal property and lived by alms.

Metropolitan   An archbishop having authority over the bishops of a province.

Official   The presiding officer in a bishop's or an archdeacon's court; the bishop's Official is often known as the Official-Principal.

Peter's Pence   An annual tribute of a penny from every householder with lands of a certain value, rendered by England to the Papacy.

Procuration   Provision of entertainment for the bishop, archdeacon or other visitor, normally commuted to a money payment.

Rector   Parson of a parish church whose revenues are not appropriated to a monastic house, etc. In an appropriated church, the monastery or other appropriating body was regarded as the corporate rector.

Regulars   Those bound by a religious rule, e.g. monks, canons, friars, nuns.

Seculars   Those clergy not bound by a religious rule, mainly those serving parishes.

Simony   The act of buying or selling an ecclesiastical office.

Suffragan   (a) A bishop subordinate to an archbishop, e.g. Bishop of London to Archbishop of Canterbury. (b) Subsidiary bishop acting as assistant to diocesan in spiritual matters.

118

Tithe The tenth part of produce, income 'etc., due for the support of the priesthood and other religious purposes.

Vicar A priest acting in a parish where the revenues are appropriated to a monastic house or other ecclesiastical corporation.

Bibliography

This bibliography is of necessity selective, and includes in the main only works to which reference is made in the text or from which documents have been selected.

PRINTED PRIMARY SOURCES

1 Bannister, A. T. (ed.), *Registrum Ricardi Mayew, Episcopi Herefordensis, A.D. MDIV-MDXVI*, Canterbury and York Society, 27 (1921).

2 Bannister, A. T. (ed.), *Registrum Caroli Bothe, Episcopi Herefordensis, A.D. MDXVI-MDXXXV*, Canterbury and York Society, 28 (1921).

3 Barker, E. E. (ed.), *The Register of Thomas Rotherham, Archbishop of York, 1480–1500*, Canterbury and York Society, 69 (1976).

4 Basing, P. (ed.), *Parish Fraternity Register: Fraternity of the Holy Trinity and SS Fabian and Sebastian in the Parish of St Botolph without Aldersgate*, London Record Society, 18 (1982).

5 *The Book of Margery Kempe*, new translation by B. Windeatt, Penguin Books, 1985.

6 Bowker, M. (ed.), *An Episcopal Court Book, 1514–1520*, Lincoln Record Society, 61 (1967).

7 *Calendar of Entries in the Papal Registers relating to Great Britain and Ireland, XIII: Papal Letters, 1471–1484*, HMSO, 1955.

8 Dickens, A. G. (ed.), *The Register or Chronicle of Butley Priory, Suffolk, 1510–1535*, Wykeham Press, Winchester, 1951.

9 Du Boulay, F. R. H., *Registrum Thome Bourgchier, Cantuariensis Archiepiscopi, A.D. 1454–1486*, Canterbury and York Society, 54 (1957).

10 Elvey, S. M. (ed.), *The Courts of the Archdeaconry of Buckingham, 1483–1523*, Buckingham Record Society, 19 (1975).

11 Fowler, J. T. (ed.), *The Rites of Durham*, Surtees Society, 107 (1903).

12 Greatrex, J. (ed.), *The Register of the Common Seal of the Priory*

of St Swithun, Winchester, 1345–1497, Hampshire Record Series 2, 1978.

13   Hamilton Thompson, A. (ed.), *Visitations of the Diocese of Lincoln, 1517–1531*, 3 vols, Lincoln Record Society, 33, 35, 37 (1940–47).

14   Harper-Bill, C. (ed.), *Register of John Morton, Archbishop of Canterbury, 1486–1500*, vol 1, Canterbury and York Society, 75 (1987).

15   Hay, D. (ed.), *The* Anglica Historia of *Polydore Vergil, A.D. 1485–1537*, Camden Society, 3rd series, 74 (1950).

16   Heath, P. (ed.), *Bishop Geoffrey Blythe's Visitations, c. 1515–1525*, Staffordshire Record Society, 4th series, 7 (1973).

17   Hilton, Walter, *The Ladder of Perfection*, trans. L. Sherley-Price, Penguin Books, 1957.

18   Howden, M. P. (ed.), *The Register of Richard Fox, Lord Bishop of Durham, 1494–1501*, Surtees Society, 147 (1932).

19   Jessopp, A. (ed.), *Visitations of the Diocese of Norwich, A.D. 1492–1532*, Camden Society, new series, 43 (1888).

20   Lyndwood, W., *Provinciale, seu Constitutiones Angliae*, London, 1679.

21   McGregor, M. (ed.), *Bedfordshire Wills Proved in the Prerogative Court of Canterbury, 1383–1548*, Bedfordshire Historical Records Society, 58 (1979).

22   Maxwell-Lyte, H. (ed.), *The Registers of Oliver King and Hadrian de Castello, Bishops of Bath and Wells, 1496–1503 and 1503–1518*, Somerset Record Society, 54 (1939).

23   Myers, A. R. (ed.), *English Historical Documents IV, 1327–1485*, Eyre and Spottiswoode, 1969.

24   Pantin, W. A. (ed.), *Documents illustrating the Activities of the General and Provincial Chapters of the English Black Monks, 1215–1540*, 3 vols, Camden Society, 3rd series, 45, 47, 54 (1931–37).

25   Sneyd, C. A. (ed.), *A Relation of the Island of England . . . about the year 1500*, Camden Society, original series, 37 (1847).

26   Sylvester, R. S. and Harding, D. P. (eds.), *Two Early Tudor Lives*, Yale University Press, 1962.

27   Williams, C. H. (ed.), *English Historical Documents V, 1485–1558*, Eyre and Spottiswoode, 1967.

28   Wood-Legh, K. L. (ed.), *Kentish Visitations of Archbishop William Warham and his Deputies, 1511–12*, Kent Archaeological Society, Kent Records 24 (1984).

29 Wright, D. P. (ed.), *The Register of Thomas Langton, Bishop of Salisbury, 1485–1493*, Canterbury and York Society, 74 (1985).

SECONDARY SOURCES: BOOKS

30 Aston, M., *Lollards and Reformers: Images and Literacy in Late Medieval Religion*, Hambledon Press, 1984.

31 Barron, C. M. and Harper-Bill, C. (eds.), *The Church in Pre-Reformation Society: Essays in Honour of F. R. H. Du Boulay*, Boydell Press, 1985.

32 Bossy, J., *Christianity in the West, 1400–1700*, Oxford University Press, 1985.

33 Bowker, M., *The Secular Clergy in the Diocese of Lincoln, 1495–1520*, Cambridge University Press, 1968.

34 Bowker, M., *The Henrician Reformation: the Diocese of Lincoln under John Longland, 1521–1547*, Cambridge University Press, 1981.

35 Brown, S., *The Medieval Courts of the York Minster Peculiar*, St Anthony's Hall, York, Borthwick Paper 66 (1984).

36 Cheney, C. R., *From Becket to Langton: English Church Government 1170–1213*, Manchester University Press, 1956.

37 Clough, C. H. (ed.), *Profession, Vocation and Culture in Later Medieval England: Essays dedicated to the memory of A. R. Myers*, Liverpool University Press, 1982.

38 Davis, J. F., *Heresy and Reformation in the South-East of England, 1520–1559*, Royal Historical Society, Studies in History 34 (1983).

39 Dickens, A. G., *The English Reformation*, Batsford, 1964.

40 Dobson, R. B. (ed.), *The Church, Politics and Patronage in the Fifteenth Century*, Alan Sutton, 1984.

41 Du Boulay, F. R. H., *An Age of Ambition: English Society in the Late Middle Ages*, Thomas Nelson, 1970.

42 Finucane, R. C., *Miracles and Pilgrims: Popular Beliefs in Medieval England*, J. M. Dent, 1977.

43 Fox, A. and Guy, J., *Reassessing the Henrician Age: Humanism, Politics and Reform, 1500–1550*, Basil Blackwell, 1986.

44 Haigh, C., *Reformation and Resistance in Tudor Lancashire*, Cambridge University Press, 1975.

45 Hamilton Thompson, A., *The English Clergy and their Organisation in the Later Middle Ages*, Oxford University Press, 1947.

46 Heath, P., *Medieval Clerical Accounts*, St Anthony's Hall, York, Borthwick Paper 26 (1964).

47 Heath, P., *The English Parish Clergy on the Eve of the Reformation*, Routledge and Kegan Paul, 1969.
48 Helmholz, R. H., *Marriage Litigation in Medieval England*, Cambridge University Press, 1974.
49 Houlbrooke, R., *Church Courts and People during the English Reformation, 1520–1570*, Oxford University Press, 1979.
50 Hudson, A., *Lollards and their Books*, Hambledon Press, 1985.
51 Hughes, J., *Pastors and Visionaries: Religion and Secular Life in Late Medieval Yorkshire*, Boydell Press, 1988.
52 Jacob, E. F., *Archbishop Henry Chichele*, Thomas Nelson, 1967.
53 Jordan, W. K., *Philanthropy in England, 1480–1660*, George Allen and Unwin, 1959.
54 Kemp, E. W., *Counsel and Consent*, SPCK, 1961.
55 Kenny, A. (ed.), *Wyclif in his Times*, Oxford University Press, 1986.
56 Knowles, M. D., *The Religious Orders in England*, vols 2, 3, Cambridge University Press, 1955–71.
57 Knowles, D., and Hadcock, R. N., *Medieval Religious Houses, England and Wales*, 2nd edn, Longman, 1971.
58 Krieder, A., *English Chantries: the Road to Dissolution*, Harvard University Press, 1979.
59 Lawrence, C. H. (ed.), *The English Church and the Papacy in the Middle Ages*, Burns and Oates, 1965.
60 Le Goff, J., *The Birth of Purgatory*, trans. A. Goldhammer, Scolar Press, 1984.
61 Logan, F. D., *Excommunication and the Secular Arm in Medieval England*, Toronto, Pontifical Institute of Medieval Studies, 1968.
62 Lunt, W. E., *The Financial Relations of the Papacy with England, 1327–1534*, Medieval Academy of America Publications 74 (1962).
63 McConica, J. K., *English Humanists and Reformation Politics*, Oxford University Press, 1965.
64 McCullough, D., *Suffolk and the Tudors: Politics and Religion in an English County, 1500–1600*, Oxford University Press, 1986.
65 McFarlane, K. B., *Lancastrian Kings and Lollard Knights*, Oxford University Press, 1972.
66 Marius, R., *Thomas More: a Biography*, J. M. Dent, 1985.
67 Moran, J-A. H., *Education and Learning in the City of York, 1300–1560*, St Anthony's Hall, York, Borthwick Paper 55 (1979).

Bibliography

68 Moran, J-A. H., *The Growth of English Schooling, 1340–1548: Learning, Literacy and Laicization in pre-Reformation York Diocese*, Princeton University Press, 1985.
69 Morris, C., *The Discovery of the Individual, 1050–1200*, SPCK, 1972.
70 Oakley, F., *The Western Church in the Later Middle Ages*, Cornell University Press, 1979.
71 O'Day, R., and Heal, F. (eds.), *Continuity and Change: Personnel and Administration of the Church in England, 1500–1642*, Leicester University Press, 1976.
72 O'Day, R., and Heal, F. (eds.), *Princes and Paupers in the English Church, 1500–1800*, Leicester University Press, 1981.
73 Orme, N., *English Schools in the Middle Ages*, Methuen, 1973.
74 Orme, N., *Exeter Cathedral as it was, 1050–1550*, Devon Books, 1986.
75 Owst, G. R., *Literature and Pulpit in Medïeval England*, 2nd edn, Basil Blackwell, 1961.
76 Pantin, W. A., *The English Church in the Fourteenth Century*, Cambridge University Press, 1955.
77 Pfaff, R. W., *New Liturgical Feasts in Later Medieval England*, Oxford University Press, 1970.
78 Platt, C., *The Abbeys and Priories of Medieval England*, Secker and Warburg, 1984.
79 Platt, C., *The Parish Churches of Medieval England*, Secker and Warburg, 1981.
80 Pollard, A. F., *Wolsey*, Longman, 1929.
81 Rosenthal, J. T., *The Purchase of Paradise*, Routledge and Kegan Paul, 1972.
82 Rubin, M., *Charity and Community in Medieval Cambridge*, Cambridge University Press, 1987.
83 Scarisbrick, J. J., *The Reformation and the English People*, Basil Blackwell, 1984.
84 Scattergood, V. J., *Politics and Poetry in the Fifteenth Century*, Blandford Press, 1971.
85 Southern, R. W., *Western Society and the Church in the Middle Ages*, Penguin Books, 1970.
86 Storey, R. L., *Diocesan Administration in Fifteenth-Century England*, 2nd edn, St Anthony's Hall, York, Borthwick Paper 16 (1972).
87 Storey, R. L., *The Reign of Henry VII*, Blandford Press, 1968.
88 Tanner, N. P., *The Church in Late Medieval Norwich, 1370–1532*, Toronto, Pontifical Institute of Medieval Studies, 1984.

124

89 Thomas, K., *Religion and the Decline of Magic: Studies in Popular Beliefs in Sixteenth- and Seventeenth-Century England*, Weidenfeld and Nicholson, 1971.

90 Thomson, J. A. F., *The Later Lollards, 1414–1520*, Oxford University Press, 1965.

91 Vale, M. G. A., *Piety, Charity and Literacy among the Yorkshire Gentry, 1370–1480*, St Anthony's Hall, York, Borthwick Paper 50 (1976).

92 Westlake, H. F., *The Parish Gilds of Mediaeval England*, SPCK, 1919.

93 Wilkie, W. E., *The Cardinal Protectors of England: Rome and the Tudors before the Reformation*, Cambridge University Press, 1974.

94 Woodcock, B. L., *Medieval Ecclesiastical Courts in the Diocese of Canterbury*, Oxford University Press, 1952.

95 Wunderli, R. M., *London Church Courts and Society on the Eve of the Reformation*, Medieval Academy of America Publications, *Speculum* Anniversary Monographs, 7, 1981.

SECONDARY SOURCES: ARTICLES AND ESSAYS

96 Armstrong, C. A. J., 'The Piety of Cicely, Duchess of York: a study in late-medieval culture', in id., *England, France and Burgundy in the Fifteenth Century*, Hambledon Press, 1983.

97 Baker, D., 'Old Wine in New Bottles: Attitudes to Reform in Fifteenth-Century England', *Studies in Church History*, 14 (1977).

98 Bittle, W. G., and Lane, T. L., 'Inflation and Philanthropy in England: a Reassessment of W. K. Jordan's Data', *Economic History Review*, 2nd series, 39 (1976).

99 Bossy, J., 'Blood and Baptism: Kinship, Community and Christianity in Western Europe from the Fourteenth to the Seventeenth Centuries', *Studies in Church History*, 10 (1973).

100 Bossy, J., 'The Social History of Confession in the Age of the Reformation', *Transactions of the Royal Historical Society*, 5th series, 25 (1975).

101 Bossy, J., 'Holiness and Society', *Past and Present*, 75 (1977).

102 Bossy, J., 'The Mass as a Social Institution, 1200–1700', *Past and Present*, 100 (1983).

103 Bowker, M., 'Some Archdeacons' Court Books and the Commons' Supplication against the Ordinaries', in Bullough, D. A., and Storey, R. L. (eds.), *The Study of Medieval Records*, Oxford University Press, 1971.

104 Bowker, M., 'The Henrician Reformation and the Parish Clergy', *Bulletin of the Institute of Historical Research*, 50 (1977).

105 Bradshaw, B., 'The Controversial Sir Thomas More', *Journal of Ecclesiastical History*, 36 (1985).

106 Brigden, S., 'Tithe Controversy in Reformation London', *Journal of Ecclesiastical History*, 32 (1981).

107 Brigden, S., 'Religion and Social Obligation in Early Sixteenth-Century London', *Past and Present*, 103 (1984).

108 Burgess, C., '"For the Increase of Divine Service": Chantries in the Parish in Late Medieval Bristol', *Journal of Ecclesiastical History*, 36 (1985).

109 Catto, J., 'Religion and the English Nobility in the Later Fourteenth Century', in Lloyd Jones, H., *et al.* (eds.), *History and Imagination: Essays in honour of H. R. Trevor Roper*, Duckworth, 1981.

110 Catto, J., 'Religious Change under Henry V', in Harriss, G. L. (ed.), *Henry V: the Practice of Kingship*, Oxford University Press, 1985.

111 Catto, J., 'John Wyclif and the Cult of the Eucharist', in Walsh, K., and Wood, D. (eds.), *The Bible in the Medieval World, Studies in Church History* Subsidia 4 (1985).

112 Cheyette, F., 'Kings, Courts, Cures and Sinecures: the Statute of Provisors and the Common Law', *Traditio*, 19 (1963).

113 Cobban, A., 'Theology and Law in the Medieval Colleges of Oxford and Cambridge', *Bulletin of the John Rylands Library*, 65 (1982).

114 Constable, G., 'Resistance to Tithes in the Middle Ages', *Journal of Ecclesiastical History*, 13 (1962).

115 Cross, C., 'York Clerical Piety and St Peter's School on the Eve of the Reformation', *York Historian*, 2 (1978).

116 Davis, V., 'The Rule of St Paul, the First Hermit, in Late Medieval England', *Studies in Church History*, 22 (1985).

117 Dickinson, J. C., 'Early Suppressions of English Houses of Austin Canons', in Ruffer, V., and Taylor, A. J., *Medieval Studies Presented to Rose Graham*, Oxford University Press, 1950.

118 Dobson, R. B., 'The Foundation of Perpetual Chantries by the Citizens of Medieval York', *Studies in Church History*, 4 (1967).

119 Du Boulay, F. R. H., 'Charitable Subsidies Granted to the

Archbishops of Canterbury, 1300–1489', *Bulletin of the Institute of Historical Research*, 23 (1950).

120 Duggan, L. G., 'The Unresponsiveness of the Late Medieval Church: a Reconsideration', *Sixteenth-Century Journal*, 9 (1978).

121 Duggan, L. G., 'Fear and Confession on the Eve of the Reformation', *Archiv für Reformationsgeschichte*, 75 (1984).

122 Dunn, E. C., 'Popular Devotion in the Vernacular Drama of Medieval England', *Medievalia et Humanistica*, 4 (1973).

123 Dunning, R. W., 'The Wells Consistory Court in the Fifteenth Century', *Proceedings of the Somerset Archaeological and Natural History Society*, 106 (1962).

124 Dunning, R. W., 'Patronage and Promotion in the Late Medieval Church', in Griffiths, R. A. (ed.), *Patronage, the Crown and the Provinces in Later Medieval England,* Alan Sutton, 1981.

125 Dunning, R. W., 'Revival at Glastonbury, 1530–39', *Studies in Church History*, 14 (1977).

126 Fines, J., 'Heresy Trials in the Diocese of Coventry and Lichfield, 1511–12', *Journal of Ecclesiastical History*, 14 (1963).

127 Fleming, P. W., 'Charity, Faith and the Gentry of Kent, 1422–1529', in Pollard, A. J. (ed.), *Property and Politics: Essays in Later Medieval English History*, Alan Sutton, 1984.

128 Frankforter, A. D., 'The Reformation and the Register: Episcopal Administration of Parishes in Late Medieval England', *Catholic Historical Review*, 63 (1977).

129 Fuggles, J. F., 'The Parish Clergy in the Archdeaconry of Leicester, 1520–1540', *Transactions of the Leicestershire Archaeological and Historical Society*, 46 (1970–1).

130 Goodman, A., 'Henry VII and Christian Renewal', *Studies in Church History*, 17 (1981).

131 Haigh, C., 'Anticlericalism and the English Reformation', *History*, 68 (1983).

132 Haines, R. M., 'Aspects of the Episcopate of John Carpenter, bishop of Worcester, 1444–1476', *Journal of Ecclesiastical History*, 19 (1968).

133 Haines, R. M., 'The Education of the English Clergy during the Later Middle Ages', *Canadian Journal of History*, 4 (1969).

134 Haines, R. M., 'The Practice and Problems of a Fifteenth-Century Bishop: The Episcopate of William Gray', *Medieval Studies*, 34 (1972).

135 Haines, R. M., 'Church, Society and Politics in the Early Fifteenth Century as viewed from an English Pulpit', *Studies in Church History*, 12 (1975).

136 Hanawalt, B. A., 'Keepers of the Lights: Late Medieval English Parish Gilds', *Journal of Medieval and Renaissance Studies*, 14 (1984).

137 Harper-Bill, C., 'A Late Medieval Visitation: the Diocese of Norwich in 1499', *Proceedings of the Suffolk Institute of Archaeology and History*, 34 (1977).

138 Harper-Bill, C., 'Archbishop John Morton and the Province of Canterbury, 1486–1500', *Journal of Ecclesiastical History*, 29 (1978).

139 Harper-Bill, C., 'Monastic Apostasy in Late Medieval England', *Journal of Ecclesiastical History*, 32 (1981).

140 Harper-Bill, C., 'John Colet's Convocation Sermon and the Pre-Reformation Church in England', *History*, 73 (1988).

141 Hay, D., 'The Church of England in the Later Middle Ages', *History*, 53 (1968).

142 Head, C., 'Pope Pius II and the Wars of the Roses', *Archivum Historiae Pontificiae*, 8 (1970).

143 Heal, F., 'The Parish Clergy and the Reformation in the Diocese of Ely', *Proceedings of the Cambridge Antiquarian Society*, 66 (1975).

144 Heal, F., 'Henry VIII and the Wealth of the English Episcopate', *Archiv für Reformationsgeschichte*, 66 (1975).

145 Helmholz, R. H., 'The Writ of Prohibition to Court Christian before 1500', *Medieval Studies*, 43 (1981).

146 Hicks, M. A., 'The Piety of Margaret Lady Hungerford (d. 1478)', *Journal of Ecclesiastical History*, 38 (1987).

147 James, M., 'Ritual, Drama and Social Body in the Late Medieval English Town', *Past and Present*, 98 (1983).

148 Johnson, A. F., 'The Gild of Corpus Christi and the Procession of Corpus Christi in York', *Medieval Studies*, 38 (1976).

149 Kaufman, P. I., 'Henry VII and Sanctuary', *Church History*, 53 (1984).

150 Keiser, G. R., 'The Holy Boke Gratia Dei', *Viator*, 12 (1981).

151 Knecht, R. J., 'The Episcopate and the Wars of the Roses', *University of Birmingham Historical Journal*, 6 (1958).

152 Knowles, M. D., 'The Case of St Albans Abbey in 1490', *Journal of Ecclesiastical History*, 3 (1951).

153 Knowles, M. D., 'The English Bishops, 1070–1532', in Watt, J. A., *et al.* (eds.), *Medieval Studies Presented to Aubrey Gwynn, S. J.*, Colm O Lochlainn, Dublin, 1961.

154 Lerner, R. E., 'The "Rich Complexity" of the Late Medieval Church', *Medievalia et Humanistica*, 12 (1984).

155 Linnell, C. L. S., 'The Commonplace Book of Robert Reynys of Acle', *Norfolk Archaeology*, 32 (1958–61).

156 Lovatt, R., 'John Blacman, Biographer of Henry VI', in Alexander, J. J. G., and Gibson, M. T. (eds.), *Medieval Learning and Literature: Studies Presented to R. W. Hunt*, Oxford University Press, 1976.

157 Lovatt, R., 'A Collector of Apocryphal Anecdotes: John Blacman Revisited', in Pollard, A. J. (ed.), *Property and Politics: Essays in Later Medieval English History*, Alan Sutton, 1984.

158 Mason, E., 'The Role of the English Parishioner, 1100–1500', *Journal of Ecclesiastical History*, 27 (1976).

159 McHardy, A. K., 'Some Late Medieval Eton College Wills', *Journal of Ecclesiastical History*, 28 (1977).

160 McHardy, A. K., 'Liturgy and Propaganda in the Diocese of Lincoln during the Hundred Years War', *Studies in Church History*, 18 (1982).

161 Moran, J-A. H., 'Clerical Recruitment in the Diocese of York, 1340–1530: Data and Commentary', *Journal of Ecclesiastical History*, 34 (1983).

162 Orme, N., 'Education and Learning at a Medieval English Cathedral: Exeter 1380–1548', *Journal of Ecclesiastical History*, 32 (1981).

163 Owen, D. M., 'Synods in the Diocese of Ely in the Later Middle Ages and the Sixteenth Century', *Studies in Church History*, 3 (1966).

164 Owen, D. M., 'Ecclesiastical Jurisdiction in England, 1300–1550: the Records and their Interpretation', *Studies in Church History*, 11 (1975).

165 Pantin, W. A., 'Instructions for a Devout and Literate Layman', in Alexander, J. J. G., and Gibson, M. T. (eds.), *Medieval Learning and Literature: Studies Presented to R. W. Hunt*, Oxford University Press, 1976.

166 Partner, P., 'The "Budget" of the Roman Church in the Renaissance Period', in Jacob, E. F. (ed.), *Italian Renaissance Studies*, Faber and Faber, 1960.

167 Pill, D. H., 'The Administration of the Diocese of Exeter

under Bishop Veysey', *Transactions of the Devon Association*, 108 (1966).

168 Plumb, D., 'The Social and Economic Spread of Rural Lollardy: a Reappraisal', *Studies in Church History*, 23 (1986).

169 Rosenthal, J. T., 'The Fifteenth-Century Episcopate: Careers and Bequests', *Studies in Church History*, 10 (1973).

170 Rubin, M., 'Corpus Christi Fraternities and Late Medieval Piety', *Studies in Church History*, 23 (1986).

171 Russell, G. H., 'Vernacular Instruction of the Laity in the Later Middle Ages in England: Some Texts and Notes', *Journal of Religious History*, 2 (1962).

172 Saul, N., 'The Religious Sympathies of the Gentry in Gloucestershire, 1200–1500', *Transactions of the Bristol and Gloucestershire Archaeological Society*, 98 (1980).

173 Scarisbrick, J. J., 'Clerical Taxation in England, 1485 to 1547', *Journal of Ecclesiastical History*, 11 (1960).

174 Schoeck, R. J., 'Canon Law in England on the Eve of the Reformation', *Medieval Studies*, 25 (1963).

175 Smith, D. M., 'Suffragan Bishops in the Medieval Diocese of Lincoln', *Lincolnshire History and Archaeology*, 17 (1982).

176 Storey, R. L., 'Recruitment of English Clergy in the Period of the Conciliar Movement', *Annuarium Historiae Conciliorum*, 7 (1977).

177 Swanson, R. N., 'Titles to Orders in Medieval English Episcopal Registers', in Mayr-Harting, H. and Moore, R. I. (eds.), *Studies in Medieval History Presented to R. H. C. Davis*, Hambledon Press, 1985.

178 Swanson, R. N., 'Universities, Graduates and Benefices in Later Medieval England', *Past and Present*, 106 (1985).

179 Thomson, J. A. F., 'Tithe Disputes in Later Medieval London', *English Historical Review*, 78 (1963).

180 Thomson, J. A. F., 'Piety and Charity in Late Medieval London', *Journal of Ecclesiastical History*, 16 (1965).

181 Underwood, M. G., 'Politics and Piety in the Household of Lady Margaret Beaufort', *Journal of Ecclesiastical History*, 38 (1987).

182 Van Engen, J., 'The Christian Middle Ages as an Historiographical Problem', *American Historical Review*, 91 (1986).

183 Wilks, M., '*Reformatio Regni*: Wyclif and Hus as Leaders of Religious Protest Movements', *Studies in Church History*, 9 (1972).

184 Wilks, M., 'Royal Patronage and Anti-Papalism from

Ockham to Wyclif', in Hudson, A. and Wilks, M. (eds.), *From Ockham to Wyclif*, Studies in Church History Subsidia 5 (1987).

185 Wood-Legh, K. L., 'Some Aspects of the History of Chantries in the Later Middle Ages', *Transactions of the Royal Historical Society*, 4th series, 28 (1946).

186 Wordsworth, C., 'On Some Pardons or Indulgences Preserved in Yorkshire, 1412–1527', *Yorkshire Archaeological Journal*, 16 (1901).

Bibliographical Update for Revised Edition

A great deal of important work has appeared since this book was written in the summer of 1988. If it were to be rewritten now, in November 1995, it would doubtless be very different in terms of the illustrative material employed, but not in the general lines of interpretation, which I feel have often been reinforced by more detailed local and regional studies. I continue to believe that the late medieval Church, in England at least, was in a healthy state and satisfied the spiritual and social aspirations of the vast majority of the English people.

With regard to those original sources on which all judgements must ultimately be based, several English calendars of Latin documents relating to the Pre-Reformation Church have lately become available. The *Calendar of Entries in Papal Registers relating to Great Britain and Ireland,* now published by the Irish Historical Manuscripts Commission, has proceeded as far as 1513. The Canterbury and York Society has produced the *Register of John Catterick, Bishop of Coventry and Lichfield, 1415–19,* ed. R. N. Swanson (1990), the second volume of the *Register of John Morton, Archbishop of Canterbury, 1486–1500,* ed. C. Harper-Bill (1991), and the *Register of John Waltham, Bishop of Salisbury, 1388–95,* ed. T. C. B. Timmins (1994). A rare record of a house of friars is presented in *The Cartulary of the Augustinian Friars of Clare,* ed. C. Harper-Bill (Suffolk Record Society, 1991). Selected account rolls from Selby abbey, Yorkshire, are translated by J. H. Tillotson, *Monastery and Society in the Late Middle Ages* (Boydell Press, 1988). A monumental work of scholarship is *English Wycliffite Sermons,* ed. A. Hudson and P. Gradon (3 vols, Oxford University Press, 1983–90), and a further group of such texts are printed in *Lollard Sermons,* ed. G. Cigman (Early English Text Society 294, 1989). A wide selection of the writings of the orthodox English mystics is contained in *English Mystics of the Middle Ages,* ed. B. Windeatt (Cambridge University Press, 1994), while R. N. Swanson has provided a very wide variety of source material in *Catholic England: Faith, Religion and Observance before the Reformation* (Manchester University Press, 1993).

Since the present book was written, several other general accounts have appeared:

C. Haigh, *English Reformations: Religion, Politics and Society under the Tudors* (Oxford University Press, 1993).
P. Heath, *Church and Realm, 1272–1461* (Fontana, 1988).
P. Heath, *The Church and the Shaping of English Society, 1215–1535* (Edward Arnold, 1995).
R. N. Swanson, *Church and Society in Later Medieval England* (Basil Blackwell, 1989, revd. edn. 1993).
J. A. F. Thomson, *The Early Tudor Church and Society, 1485–1529* (Longman, 1993).

Four previously published and nine new essays, on a wide range of topics, are included in R. M. Haines, *Ecclesia Anglicana: Studies in the English Church of the Later Middle Ages* (Toronto University Press, 1989). Special mention should be made of an earlier work too little known on this side of the Atlantic: P. I. Kaufman, *The 'Polytyque Church': Religion and Early Tudor Political Culture, 1485–1516* (Mercer University Press, Macon, Georgia, 1986), which details the efforts of the English episcopate to achieve institutional reform within the context of a Church which was national but utterly and orthodoxly Catholic. A much-needed survey of the wider European context is provided by R. N. Swanson, *Religion and Devotion in Europe, c. 1215 – c. 1515* (Cambridge University Press, 1995), while a good general account of the whole history of the medieval institution is J. H. Lynch, *The Medieval Church: A Brief Account* (Longman, 1992).

The most important book to be published in recent years on the religion of late medieval and Tudor England is probably E. Duffy, *The Stripping of the Altars: Traditional Religion in England, 1400–1580* (Yale University Press, 1992). A remarkable and detailed, if for some controversial, study of parochial religion which puts flesh on the bones of the so-called 'revisionist' interpretation of the English Reformation. A further wide-ranging study of parochial religion is provided by B. Kümin, *The Shaping of a Community: The Rise and Reformation of the English Parish, c. 1400–1560* (Edward Arnold, St Andrew's Studies in Reformation History, 1995), which contains the first quantitative analysis of churchwardens' accounts on a national scale. R. Whiting, *The Blind Devotion of the People: Popular Religion and the English Reformation* (Cambridge University Press, 1989) is a study based on

Devon and Cornwall, where it is demonstrated that enthusiasm for religion before the Reformation gave way to torpor and apathy thereafter. The Pre-Reformation Church in the capital (where the situation may have been rather different from the rest of the country, in that the concept of 'anticlericalism' has not been entirely demolished) is surveyed in the early pages of S. Brigden, *London and the Reformation* (Oxford University Press, 1989). A longer regional view is taken by A. D. Brown, *Popular Piety in Late Medieval England: The Diocese of Salisbury, 1250–1550* (Oxford University Press, 1995). R Hutton, *The Rise and Fall of Merry England* (Oxford University Press, 1994) examines annual festivals celebrated both nationally and regionally, and the effect of the Reformation upon them.

The central mystery of the Catholic Church is studied by M. Rubin, Corpus Christi: *The Eucharist in Late Medieval Culture* (Cambridge University Press, 1991). H. L. Spencer, *English Preaching in the Late Middle Ages* (Oxford University Press, 1993) reveals how the vernacular was used from the late fourteenth century to explore ideas hitherto expressed in Latin. Religious drama is studied by G. McT. Gibson, *The Theater of Devotion: East Anglian Drama and Society in the Late Middle Ages* (Chicago University Press, 1989). The impact of plague on the English Church and religion is studied in broad terms by C. Harper-Bill in *The Black Death in England, 1348–1500*, ed. P. Lindley and M. Ormrod (Paul Watkins Press, 1995), and in detail for the diocese of Hereford by W. Dohar, *The Black Death and Pastoral Leadership* (Pennsylvania University Press, 1995). Several essays in *Death in Towns, AD 100–1600* (Leicester University Press, 1992) deal with late medieval England, and commemoration of the dead is treated in two articles derived from significant theses: R. Dinn, ' "Monuments Answerable to Men's Worth": Burial Patterns, Social Status and Gender in Late-Medieval Bury St Edmunds', *Journal of Ecclesiastical History*, 46 (1995), and J. Middleton-Stewart, 'The Provision of Books for Church Use in the Deanery of Dunwich, 1370–1547', *Proceedings of Suffolk Institute of Archaeology*, 38 (1994).

A volume of essays edited by S. J. Wright, *Parish, Church and People: Local Studies in Lay Religion, 1350–1750* (Routledge, 1988), contains essays by C. Burgess on perceptions of Purgatory in late medieval England and by G. Rosser on communities of parish and guild. Burgess studies 'Late Medieval Wills and Pious Convention' in *Profit, Piety and the Professions in Later Medieval England* (Alan Sutton, 1990), and also, with B. Kümin, 'Penitential Bequests and

Parish Regimes in Late Medieval England' in *Journal of Ecclesiastical History*, 44 (1993). The papers delivered at a day conference on 'The Christian Life in the Late Middle Ages' are printed in *Transactions of the Royal Historical Society*, 6th series, 1: J. Bossy on 'Prayers', R. B. Dobson on 'English Monastic Cathedrals', G. Rosser on 'Parochial Conformity and Popular Religion' and R. G. Davis on 'Lollardy and Locality'. An original approach is adopted by N. Orme, 'Children and the Church in Medieval England', *Journal of Ecclesiastical History*, 45 (1994).

A detailed study of Anglo-Papal relations is provided by M. Harvey, *England, Rome and the Papacy, 1417–64* (Manchester University Press, 1993). The Papacy continued to preach and organise crusades, albeit now defensive, and the English response is examined by C. Tyerman, *England and the Crusades, 1095–1588* (Chicago University Press, 1988). In the important field of Roman canon law and the practice of the ecclesiastical courts, a much needed general survey is provided by J. A. Brundage, *Medieval Canon Law* (Longman, 1995), while D. M. Owen, *The Medieval Canon Law: Teaching and Transmission* (Cambridge University Press, 1990) exploits particularly the rich archives of Ely and Lincoln dioceses. The important papers of R. H. Helmholz are collected in *Canon Law and the Law of England* (Hambledon Press, 1987), and Helmholz has also studied the changes of the sixteenth century in *Roman Canon Law in Reformation England* (Cambridge University Press, 1990).

A great deal of valuable work on ecclesiastical institutions in England has appeared in recent years. The cathedrals in general have been treated by S. E. Lehmberg, *The Reformation of Cathedrals: Cathedrals and English Society, 1485–1603* (Princeton University Press, 1988) and by D. Lepine, *A Brotherhood of Canons Serving God: English Secular Cathedrals in the Later Middle Ages* (Boydell Press, 1995). Among studies of particular cathedrals, which all contain material on the late middle ages, are *A History of Lincoln Minster*, ed. D. M. Owen (Cambridge University Press, 1994); *Coventry's First Cathedral*, ed. G. Demidowicz (Paul Watkins Press, 1994); *A History of Canterbury Cathedral*, ed. P. Collinson *et al.* (Oxford University Press, 1995); and *Norwich Cathedral, 1096–1996: Church, City and Diocese*, ed. I. Atherton *et al.* (Hambledon Press, 1996). An important essay is J. Greatrex, 'The English Cathedral Priories and the Pursuit of Learning in the Later Middle Ages', *Journal of Ecclesiastical History*, 45 (1994). A lesser collegiate church is studied by P. Coulstock, *The Collegiate Church of Wimborne Minster* (Boydell Press, 1993).

Much has appeared on the English universities. An excellent general study is A. B. Cobban, *The Medieval English Universities: Oxford and Cambridge to c. 1500* (University of California Press, 1988). The individual universities are studied by R. Leader, *A History of the University of Cambridge*, i, *The University to 1546* (Cambridge University Press, 1988) and in two volumes of *The History of the University of Oxford*: ii, *Later Medieval Oxford*, ed. J. I. Catto and R. Evans; iii, *The Collegiate University*, ed. J. McConica (Oxford University Press, 1992, 1986). There has been a recent renewal of interest in the history of hospitals; see especially N. Orme and M. Webster, *The English Hospital, 1070–1570* (Yale University Press, 1995); C. Rawcliffe, *The Hospitals of Medieval Norwich* (University of East Anglia, 1995), and P. H. Cullum, *Cremetts and Corrodies: Care of the Poor and Sick at St Leonard's Hospital, York, in the Middle Ages* (Borthwick Institute, York, 1991).

The general neglect of monasticism in recent decades has been partially remedied. B. F. Harvey, *Living and Dying in England, 1100–1500: The Monastic Experience* (Oxford University Press, 1993), applies monastic evidence, especially from Westminster, to wider social and economic issues. Patronage is studied by B. Thompson, 'Monasteries and their Patrons at Foundation and Dissolution', *Transactions of the Royal Historical Society*, 6th series, 4 (1994). Two individual Yorkshire houses are treated in J. H. Tillotson, *Marrick Priory: A Nunnery in Late Medieval Yorkshire* and J. Burton, *Kirkham Priory from Foundation to Dissolution* (Borthwick Institute, York, 1989, 1995), while northern institutions, both monastic and secular, are examined in the collected essays of R. B. Dobson, *Church and Society in the Medieval North of England* (Hambledon Press, 1995). A regional study of female monasticism is provided by R. Gilchrist and M. Oliva, *Religious Women in Medieval East Anglia* (University of East Anglia, 1993), while Y. Parry examines the religious life of the early sixteenth-century nuns of Amesbury in *Historical Research*, 67 (1994). Monastic spirituality and its wider implications are examined in two articles in *Journal of Ecclesiastical History*, 43 (1992): R. Lovatt, 'The Library of John Blacman and Contemporary Carthusian Spirituality', and J. T. Rhodes, 'Syon Abbey and its Religious Publications in the Sixteenth Century'. There are several papers relevant to this period in the two volumes of *Monastic Studies*, ed. J. Loades (Headstart History, 1990, 1991).

Various short studies of the secular clergy recently published include: R. N. Swanson, 'Problems of the Priesthood in Pre-

Reformation England', *English Historical Review*, 105 (1990); V. Davis, 'Rivals for Ministry? Ordination of Secular and Religious Clergy in Southern England, c. 1300–1500', *Studies in Church History*, 26 (1989); and R. L. Storey, 'Ordination of Secular Priests in Early Tudor London', *Nottingham Medieval Studies*, 33 (1989).

A number of full-scale studies of notable individuals have appeared. The reputation of one bishop is enhanced by V. Davis, *William Wayneflete: Bishop and Educationalist* (Boydell Press, 1993), while R. B. Gleeson, *John Colet* (University of California Press, 1989) seeks to diminish that of the famous Dean of St Paul's. There have been two studies of John Fisher, a volume of essays treating most aspects of his career, *Humanism, Reform and the Reformation: The Career of Bishop John Fisher*, ed. B. Bradshaw and E. Duffy (Cambridge, 1989), and R. Rex, *The Theology of John Fisher* (Cambridge University Press, 1991). P. Gwyn, *The King's Cardinal: The Rise and Fall of Thomas Wolsey* (Barrie and Jenkin, 1990), has generally been regarded as over-favourable to Wolsey, although there is much to be said for the view that, like Morton before him, he sought ecclesiastical reform through centralisation; but a more rounded picture is inevitably presented in the various essays in *Cardinal Wolsey: Church, State and Art*, ed. S. Gunn and P. Lindley (Cambridge University Press, 1991). Two extremely influential lay persons are examined in M. K. Jones and M. G. Underwood, *The King's Mother: Lady Margaret Beaufort, Countess of Richmond and Derby* (Cambridge University Press, 1992), and L. L. Martz, *Thomas More: The Search for the Inner Man* (Yale University Press, 1990).

So much for the orthodox. There have appeared several distinguished studies of the small Lollard minority. The considered conclusions of a textual scholar are presented in A. Hudson, *The Premature Reformation: Wycliffite Texts and Lollard History* (Oxford University Press, 1989), while a longer view is taken by M. Aston, *England's Iconoclasts: Laws against Images* (Oxford University Press, 1988). Dr Aston has also provided a second volume of collected essays, *Faith and Fire: Popular and Unpopular Religion, 1350–1600* (Hambledon Press, 1993), and has studied a particularly significant incident in 'Iconoclasm at Rickmansworth, 1522: Troubles of Churchwardens', *Journal of Ecclesiastical History*, 40 (1989). A particularly important article is J. A. F. Thomson, 'Orthodox Religion and the Origins of Lollardy', *History*, 74 (1989).

Finally, two volumes of collected papers concentrate exclusively or partly on many aspects of the late medieval Church in England:

Religious Belief and Ecclesiastical Careers in Late Medieval England, ed. C. Harper-Bill (Boydell Press, 1991), and *Medieval Ecclesiastical Studies in Honour of Dorothy M. Owen*, ed. M. J. Franklin and C. Harper-Bill (Boydell Press, 1995). There are, too, many articles not specifically mentioned above in recent issues of the various historical journals, especially the *Journal of Ecclesiastical History* and *Studies in Church History*.

Index